Annie's Garden Journal

Annie's Garden Journal

Reflections on Roses, Weeds, Men, and Life.

Annie Spiegelman

A Birch Lane Press Book
Published by Carol Publishing Group

A Birch Lane Press Book
Published by Carol Publishing Group
Birch Lane Press is a registered trademark of Carol Communications, Inc.

Editorial, sales and distribution, rights and permissions inquiries should be
addressed to Carol Publishing Group, 120 Enterprise Avenue, Secaucus,
N.J. 07094

In Canada: Canadian Manda Group, One Atlantic Avenue, Suite 105,
Toronto, Ontario M6K 3E7

Carol Publishing Group books may be purchased in bulk at special discounts
for sales promotion, fund-raising, or educational purposes. Special editions
can be created to specifications. For details, contact Special Sales
Department, 120 Enterprise Avenue, Secaucus, N.J. 07094.

Monthly floral decorations by Margaret Wolf

Manufactured in the United States of America
10 9 8 7 6 5 4 3 2 1

Library of Congress Cataloging-in-Publication Data
Spiegelman, Annie.
    Annie's garden journal : reflections on roses, weeds, men, and
life / Annie Spiegelman.
        p.   cm.
    "A Birch Lane Press book."
    ISBN 1-55972-373-4 (hc)
    1. Gardening—California.   2. Gardens—California.   3. Spiegelman,
Annie.   I. Title.
SB455.S815   1996
818'.5403—dc20
    [B]   96-24046
                                                                 CIP

*This book is dedicated to my Parents
with gratitude, compassion, and love.*

I am grateful to my editor, Jim Ellison, for his expertise, hard work, and friendship. I also would like to thank Liisa O'Maley for believing in this project since day one, and for being so supportive during the entire process.

A special thanks to Robert Harrington at the Children's Garden of California, and to the Reverend Cecil Williams and Janice Mirikitani at Glide Memorial Church. These two Bay Area organizations so devoted to healing our children and communities were the catalyst in having this journal published.

And finally, thank you to my sisters Carol, Sharon, and Augusta, for understanding me with just one look and no words spoken, and most of all for always making me laugh.

For Bill

There is always something to do. There are hungry people to feed, naked people to clothe, sick people to comfort and make well. And while I don't expect you to save the world, I do think it's not asking too much for you to love those with whom you sleep, share the happiness with those whom you call friend, engage those among you who are visionary, and remove from your life those who offer you depression, despair, and disrespect.

— Nikki Giovanni

Annie's Garden Journal

September

SEPTEMBER 10

My mother's rosebushes were her only peaceful childhood memory. When she was twelve years old, the Persian gypsy next door gave her four bare-root tea roses. In the slums of Haifa, among the rodents and trash, she planted her rose garden. During the summer of her fourteenth birthday, while her roses were in full bloom, her brothers ripped each plant out, root by root, until the only thing left was my mother crying on the ground, surrounded by strewn rose petals of red, pink, white, and yellow.

At sunset, when her father came home, she was still lying in her garden, staring at the heavens above her. She was praying that someday she would run far away and never come back. He dragged her inside the house and beat her for inciting her brothers.

Next week is my mom's birthday. Sixty-something. I don't see much of my mother these days. When I do visit, I come home with the latest battle scars. First I feel my own pain and then I feel her pain. I'm planting a Peace rose today for her. My dream is that we both find peace one day, if not on the outside, then inside ourselves. This pink-yellow rose was named the Peace rose by the Americans as an emblem of hope during World War II.

The know-it-all French guy at the nursery was going on about how easy roses are to grow. He spoke English with such an irritating French accent that I hardly heard what he was saying. I kept staring at him in amazement and wondering if he was faking. Plus, I know that roses are not so simple. They need a lot of attention. They want sunshine, lots of water, good food, and love. Then they'll be happy and healthy; smiling and blooming proudly.

I try not to be too skeptical in the garden, but it's hard. First, because I'm from New York and second, because Bill and I are notorious for our bust garden. We are slaves to our garden. Sometimes we're proud parents, but most of the time we're exhausted and frustrated. I just want the stupid seeds to look like the flowers on the package they came in. Is that too much to ask? I waited almost two weeks before I planted Ma's rosebush. I didn't want to be in my usual cynical garden mode. I was waiting for the right, positive moment to plant it. Today is the day. I spoke to my mother and neither of us hung up on the other. Today is a miracle.

Roses are called the Queen of the Flowers. My sisters, Sharon, Carol, and Augusta or as I refer to them, Sha, Ca, and Ga, call our Mother the Queen Bee. If you met her, you'd know why. We are the drones trying to please her or stay out of the line of fire. My sanctuary is my garden.

I decided to keep a garden journal. That way I could keep track of what the hell was going on out here and maybe I'd be a better gardener or become a better person. I was excited about my journal idea. I told Bill we had to document every single new finding in the yard. We need to update and record anytime we fertilize, prune, or spray; make a watering schedule; list plants that flourish and ones that die on us; and basically treat the garden as a long-term science experiment. I told him that we would learn from this and our garden would someday be spectacular!

He said, "That's nice, babe."

It took me a long time to dig the hole for that Peace rose. I felt anything but peaceful. I mixed in the compost, peat moss, and all-purpose fertilizer. Then I soaked the hole with water, put in mulch, built a cone of soil, aligned the bud union exactly two inches above the ground, spread out the roots, and mounded the soil eight inches around the plant for protection. I actually read the directions! (This is all new to me.) I only did it so that if I'm questioned by Bill, I can say, "Yes, I read the directions," and give a big sigh like it was a stupid question. Some of our most passionate arguments have been in and about the garden. Bill thinks the reason our garden is so boring is because we don't know what we're doing.

He's so negative.

After I had it planted, I looked at the picture of the beautiful Peace rose and then down at the newly planted stub of a rose-bush. I begged it to bloom. I hugged and kissed it and said I'd always be there. Then I told it the three-seasons-and-you're-out rule. I hope it got the message. After I finished that project I collapsed on the red bench and disturbed our two cats, Maui and Max. In my next life I want to come back as one of my cats. They basically pretend we don't exist. They sit like two bumps on a log and watch us work for hours in the yard. They're probably wondering, along with the entire neighborhood, why we work so hard in the garden and it still looks like hell.

SEPTEMBER 13

Today I turned down work on a local film project. I feel good about it. The script was extremely violent, and I'm trying to help mend the world. (Also, the money wasn't so hot, so I'm really not such a great person.) I have a love-hate relationship with the film business. One day I'm out in some sunny, beautiful location with wonderful, interesting people, feeling blessed to be getting paid to have so much fun. Then, the next project will be filled with greedy, egotistical lunatics who have sold their souls to the devil and look at me as if there is something very wrong because I still have a conscience. This is all very disturbing.

Instead, I took a long walk in Golden Gate Park with Bill's sister, Denise. First we went to the Rhododendron Garden. The place is so unreal. It's like being in *Lost in Space.* The plants look like man-eaters. Big, blooming rhododendrons surrounded by man-eating foxgloves. If only my shade garden looked an eighth as good as this. Denise rambled on about all her investments and business ventures while I stared in awe at the plants. That's why she's the rich one and I'm still struggling.

Next we walked over to the Rose Garden. I remember four
years ago, when my mother had come out to visit me for three
days before she went to Southern California to visit my twin sister, Ca. Ma and I would meet each morning for breakfast and
then walk through the park to the Rose Garden. We would sit
on a park bench and watch the people. We became the Rose Garden police. We made up stories and decided who could come visit
the rose garden and who were just plain losers. We laughed at
the man with the two grotesque little Pekingese kick-dogs. We
stopped and smelled each and every rose. We made fun of the
names: Rise 'n Shine, White Lightnin', Ole, Cupcake, Choo-
Choo Centennial, and, our favorite, Pink Grootendorst. It was
the last time I saw her walking pain-free. Nowadays she walks a
block or two and needs to rest. It scares me to death. This par-
ticular visit was unique for both of us. It was one of the few times
that I didn't have to share her with my attention-stealing sisters.
We took pictures of each other on the cable cars and had tea at
the Ritz-Carlton, where, of course, she complained to the head
waiter that the bread was stale. He looked down at us and, in a
crusty English accent, said, "Madame, the cucumber sandwiches
are delicately toasted, not stale." When he walked away, we
laughed like teenagers. She actually treated me like her friend.
You see, when I'm together with all my sisters and Ma, we all
seem to regress to our dysfunctional childhood roles and I just
get quiet and sad. But that trip, having Ma to myself, I was loud
and happy.

I was jerked back to the present when Denise said she had a
client to meet. She left me in the Rose Garden. I saw the sun was
peeking through the fog and I could hear my mother's laughter
in the air. I sat on a park bench near a tai chi class and closed my
eyes. I went back to last spring, when my three sisters (Sha, Ca,
and Ga), and I visited Ma in Texas. A strange thing happened.
I think I was having a mini-nervous breakdown, but I'm not
sure. I don't know what those feel like, but this was pretty bad.
I had just finished working on some superficial, useless TV movie
and I was burned out. On the last night in Dallas, it was my turn

to sleep in Ma's room. We tossed coins each night to see who had to sleep with the Queen Bee snorer. All of us dainty girls snore, but Ma scores the highest. During that visit, I was reading *The House of the Spirits*. That was the book that changed my life. It sparked interest in my own family's past history. Ma did her rounds and kissed us each goodnight, ending in her room. We talked quietly for about forty-five minutes. Then I started sobbing and shaking. I couldn't stop. Tears poured out of me all over the sheets. They wouldn't stop. Ma looked scared to death, but she kept trying to make jokes and make me laugh. I couldn't laugh. I kept saying "Don't leave me" and "Why do you have to die?" She said she would live forever so we could continue fighting. In my real life that would bother me, but that night it just made me cry and miss her more. She must have thought I had lost my mind. She held my hand until I finally fell asleep. Those tears sent me swimming into the darkness of my soul and I began a long period where old, disturbing memories slowly surfaced. I had worked so hard to cover up and forget them over the years. They have some nerve coming out when I least expect them.

I woke up the next morning drained but basically normal. I wondered if my sisters had heard any of it. I doubt it, because I think Sha would have come in. She always protects me like a good big sister. I think that was one of the most intimate hours I ever spent with my mother, and I'm sure she was exhausted from it too. I was glad to get on the plane back to San Francisco. I waved to Ma as she took the ritualistic ugly-architecture-airport-photo of us leaving. She looked a little more concerned than usual. I'm sure once the plane took off, she looked at my oldest sister Ga and said, "What did I bring up, a nut?"

I snapped back to the present when a Girl Scout troop came running through the Rose Garden singing "Miss Mary Mack," a song my nerdy sisters and I sang over and over years ago.

When I got home, I brought in some yellow roses for the table. I made a vase of them for Bill's office too. I thought about him a lot today. I thought about how angry and cynical I was before I met him. Now, I'm just cynical. But I do believe in love. We've been together now for six years. We recently brought up the idea of marriage. It made us sick. So, we vowed that we would talk about it next year, on January 1. That gives us a few months to think about talking about it. Now that Bonnie Raitt, my idol, got married, I find the institution of marriage almost acceptable. Still, whenever I think about getting married, I cry—a sure sign of something not right. Marriage to me means my parents fighting and then my father leaving. The war in our house went on for many years. Children feel and hear everything. There are no secrets. Our home was filled with love, interlaced with confusion, pain, heartbreak, and flying plastic fruit.

SEPTEMBER 17

First thing this morning, I sprinkled wildflower seeds all around the rim of the vegetable garden. Then I planted a plethora of bulbs! I love, love, love bulbs because any idiot can grow them. You really can't go wrong. From these little round lumps you plant in the fall, come amazing, magical flowers in the spring. It works even for us city chicks! Tulips, daffodils, Iris, watsonia, hyacinths, freesias, ranunculus, and crocus. I also bought an unusual lily because it was from Belgium. I remember the time my family visited Belgium. It was freezing. I don't see how any flowers grow there. Seeing the neighborhood where my father grew up brought to life all the horrifying stories we heard of the Nazi occupation.

My father is from Antwerp, Belgium. He has a beautiful sister, Ceil. When my dad was ten years old, he, my Grandpa Max and Grandma Rose, along with my Aunt Ceil, finally escaped the German occupation on a train from Brussels to France. They later fled to Spain and eventually took a boat to Cuba. This was their second attempt at fleeing their home. Their first attempt to escape was a year earlier, where they hid in an abandoned house outside the French town of Fruges. Tricked by German propaganda that Belgium was returning back to normal, my father's family made it's way back to Antwerp. Once back home they found things were not improving but slowly getting worse and more terrifying. One day on a street corner in Antwerp, Grandpa Max was heard berating the Germans by an undercover Gestapo agent. The Nazi's words were simply "You are under arrest, dirty Jew." As a trolley came by Max jumped on board, turned and kicked the Gestapo agent in the groin. By the time Max returned home, it became known that a search was on for him. The family was told to pack immediately. The children said farewell to their grandparents, Wolf and Sura, who decided to stay instead of making such a long, dangerous journey.

The next morning, wearing several layers of clothes and carrying no luggage, they made their second and final attempt to flee the Nazis. They crawled through clearings between machine gun towers during the night and hid in haystacks during the day, as search patrols came by. The goal was to reach the coast of Spain, where they could find a water route to Cuba, unlike most other countries in the Western Hemisphere, including the United States, had not closed their gates to European refugees. After various frightening setbacks and a highly paid smuggler, they finally made it to Nice and soon after to the town of Bilbao, in the Basque country of Spain. Here the family learned that the only place to get valid documents and official travel authorization was in Madrid, so Grandpa Max left his family for Madrid. On the train, he was arrested by the Guardia Civil for having no travel papers. While waiting for an officer to appear to interrogate him, he bragged about his American cigarettes and gave the soldiers two packs each. They had been smoking their own rolled cigarettes with flimsy paper and the poorest cut of tobacco. As the soldiers sat happily smoking at the train station, inhaling their brand new choice cigarettes, Grandpa Max snuck back aboard the train and made it to Madrid. Here he paid astronomically for four tickets on the "Isla de Tenerife," sailing out of Barcelona. He reunited with his family and they finally made it to Cuba. To this day, when I complain about the repugnant tobacco industry, my father always reminds me that his freedom was bought with four packs of cigarettes.

Every Hanukkah, Grandpa Max, who strongly believed in defending human rights, would pull out his atlas and highlight the escape route through Europe. All the grandkids would be circled around him and he would tell the same terrifying story each year. Transport Number XIV. This was the transport, or cattle wagon, that took our great-grandparents, Wolf and Sura, to the gas chambers at Auschwitz. They were violently dragged from their home on October 24, 1942, and piled into a railcar with fifty other Jews. They had no food or water for two days. The railcar was locked. Anyone trying to escape was shot. Wolf and Sura were seen two days later arriving at the camp but never heard of again. The meticulous Nazi records, that my father recently investigated, showed that on the day of my great grandparent's arrival the medical officer entered into his diary: "Dante's Hell seems to be a bit of a farce compared to this." The next day he wrote, "Today, wonderful autumn weather, went on bike ride to Budy via Roisko. Wilhelm back from his trip to Croatia. (Plum brandy!)"

SEPTEMBER 19

Unfortunately, I had to leave my garden this week. I'm on location working with Barbara Eden, Jeannie of *I Dream of*. Funny that such a sexist show was one of my favorite childhood programs. My sisters and I were totally in love with *I Dream of Jeannie* and *Bewitched*. Barbara is great. Just like you'd hoped Jeannie would be. I have one more week to go before returning home. Every night I sit and look at the picture of Bill near my bed. It's one I took when we were on vacation in Silverton, Colorado, a

few years ago. He is wearing his brand-new, deep purple raincoat. He's not happy though. He was just beginning his chiropractic practice and was struggling so hard to get it off the
ground. He had discovered he had to run it as a business, but he
just wanted to be a healer. It was a rude awakening.

Anyway, even though it's a sad photo, it brings back pleasant
memories. It was my first camping trip through the Southwest.
I learned how to build a fire, set up a tent, use a compass, and
read a topographical map. For a girl from New York City, that's
a big deal. That drizzly day in Silverton we were searching in the
cemetery for someone Bill had never known. My sister Ga's husband, Bob, had been buried there a year earlier. She was still living in Texas and hadn't gone to see his grave. I think the pain
was too much for her. She had loved Bob like I love Bill, deeply.
We tramped through that cemetery, in the pouring rain, for at
least an hour calling, "Ol' Dead Bob? Where are you?" We finally found him, just as the sun came out and made a rainbow.
We laid down some flowers and took a picture of his stone to send
to my sister.

The camera jammed.

I guess Bob didn't want her to see him yet.

One other time I dragged Bill to a cemetery to the grave of
someone he had never met—Fluffy, our childhood dog for four-
teen years. Fluffy was a mix of golden retriever and cocker
spaniel. He was born in France, but we didn't hold that against
him or even admit it. He died of cancer one summer while water
skiing with Ca. Ca and I were his twin mothers. We flew him between California and New York every half year. We spoiled him
outrageously. After dating Bill for three months, I asked him to
take me to Lake Tahoe to visit old dead Fluffy. We went to his
grave. On that beautiful summer day I had happy thoughts. Later
we went to the veterinarian who had put Fluffy to sleep to ask
for his medical files. Well, I just about lost it. After five years, they
throw out the animal files!! I yelled at her, "How dare you throw
out Fluffy's files? Just who do you think you are?"

We drove home in silence.

I had only been dating Bill a few months. I'm sure he was wondering what he was doing with someone so hung up on her old dead dog.

SEPTEMBER 24

When I came home from work today, Bill was out in the yard checking up on things. He thinks I plant things too close together. He may be right. I simply don't believe that the plants are going to grow. I'm too skeptical. He frowned and told me: "No more jasmine, no more potato vine, no more roses, no more crape myrtle." I guess I did go a little overboard. I can't help it. Anything that's beginning to bloom, I'll buy.

Well, . . . I guess we'll have Bill's Garden Rules from now on. Just who does he think he is?

We decided to try growing lettuces all year round. We're supposed to be able to here in this climate. Maybe it'll really work. I'm extra cynical today because my little bumpkin melon bit the dust. It had flowered and had two little round melon balls on it. I guess the neighborhood cats had a gathering here last night and squashed it to death. So sad to have made it this far and . . . At least I had nothing to do with it. Bill gave it the ceremonial burial toss into the compost pile. Then we had a contest to see who could throw the bad pear apples, from the farthest point, into the compost pile. Bill always wins, but I did pretty well. I've really improved my swing since the dead-fern toss last year.

We waited for dusk and then did a nature walk around the yard. It was pretty uneventful. In fact, my mother's Peace rose looks exactly the same as it did three weeks ago. We practically ripped it apart looking for some new growth. We finished our walk agreeing that it was a bust, but at least we had a great homegrown salad for dinner. We ate under the plum tree. My girlfriend, Ellen, gave us a beautiful birdhouse that hangs on the plum tree. It's been up for a year and we haven't had one lousy bird come visit. Another bust. We ate and tried to think of more things to be miserable about. Max, the cat, is always an easy target. We named him after Grandpa, but they're nothing like each other. We almost returned Max to the Humane Society because he was such a terror when he was a kitten. He fought with all the other backyard cats and he bit and scratched us. Then one day he just changed. He got mushy and cozy and nice. Now we put up with him, and, sometimes, when no one else is around, I even tell him I love him.

SEPTEMBER 25

Last night I had dinner with my best girlfriends, Elissa, Gwyneth, Cat, Pucci, Ellen, and Cecily. That afternoon I had been to a N.O.W. meeting (or N.O.C., as Bill calls it, National Organization of Chicks), and I was all fired up. Congresswoman Lynn Woolsley was the guest speaker. She hit on some of my favorite topics: a right to choose, domestic violence, sexual harassment, medical research, and child care. At dinner we talked about the fact that so many women are afraid to call themselves feminists even though they believe everything we stand for. A bunch of wimps out there. Afraid that their boyfriends won't like them anymore! What the hell is so frightening about the F word? Ooh, scary word! Who do they think got them the right to vote (it only took the suffragists seventy years), the right to have a car or house loan, the right to an education, a job, healthcare, child care, and child support? Our mothers and grandmothers weren't born with these rights. Somebody had to fight for them. If you believe in a woman's civil rights, in her right to be treated as an equal, then you are a feminist. You don't have to hate men anymore. That's outdated. You can love them, wear lipstick, and even wax your legs. Isn't that nice?

I came home all fired up for a hot debate with Bill. But he knows me too well and he simply agreed with everything I said, so he could get back to Monday night football.

SEPTEMBER 27

I can't stand annuals. I have much more respect for perennials. But sometimes you just need annuals. I gave in and planted a bunch at the front border of the house. It looked so plain and boring that I just got desperate and wanted quick color. I planted snapdragons, stock, Iceland poppies, and impatiens. These are "supposed" to bloom for the next few months. Yeah. Right.

The only annual that I really love is *helianthus,* or sunflower. We have a Lemon Queen and a few Autumn Beauties in the backyard near the vegetables. Up front we have a Valentine sunflower. I love this one because it's turned into a small bush with lots of lemon-colored flowers. Sunflowers are easy so they rate high around here. Anything that blooms without us threatening it gets our respect and admiration.

SEPTEMBER 29

When I first began this garden journal, I wanted to document when and what I planted, when I fertilized, and when I pruned; which plants made it, which plants went bust, and what bloomed and when; what I loved, what I hated, what got on my nerves, and what was the easiest thing to grow yet looked complicated, so that I looked extremely skilled.

I guess I've gone off on tangents, but that's the intriguing thing about a garden. It sends you off into other worlds. You find other parts of your personality, even some good ones. You learn to be patient and look forward to simple surprises in the midst of everyday chaos.

SEPTEMBER 30

I had a dreadful nightmare last night. I woke up at 3:00 A.M. in a cold sweat. I dreamed that Bill and I were hiking on the cliffs around Muir Beach. When we got to the top, he asked me to marry him.

I looked at him as if he'd gone mad.

Then I pushed him.

October

OCTOBER 2

This morning I planted a row of elephant garlic. I cook everything with lots of garlic. Elissa tells me my skin smells like a combination of garlic and gardenia oil, depending what day it is. I
guess that's what best friends are for. In honor of my grand-
mother, Safta, in Israel, I am a true garlic addict.

When my sisters and I were very young, we went to visit my
grandparents in Israel. It was the first time we had met my
mother's parents. Safta and Saba had married at age sixteen.
They had my mother, their first child, the next year. Saba was a
tyrant and Safta was strong. But afraid. When we visited them
we were too young to realize how poor and how crazy they were.
In fact, some of the fondest memories from my childhood are of
them. We'd sit in Safta's kitchen every afternoon chopping garlic, garlic, and then more garlic. Before we fixed dinner for the
big, fat men with smelly undershirts on, Safta would bathe us.
We would sit on a cracked wooden stool as she washed our hair
and told us passionate life stories in Hebrew. I never understood
the whole story, and it was freezing, but just watching her facial
expressions and hearing her laugh made it all worthwhile. My
mother would translate the stories later when she tucked us in
bed. The theme was always the same: It's a man's world.

At dinner, my sisters and I and my aunts served the men. It
was actually quite nauseating, when I think about it now. I think
our dog, Fluffy, got more respect than my mother and her sisters. My grandfather, Saba, loved his sons, and they were all that
mattered. He would call his daughters "whores" and tell them
they served no purpose.

After dinner we would play "team work" with Saba. My sisters and I would be in our pajamas and we would chase our

grandfather around the house. Then he would chase us. We would run around that house screaming while Fluffy chased us, barking like a mad dog. If you were caught, you'd be smothered with wet kisses by Saba's white, scratchy face and yell for team work. Then the sisterhood would attack and we'd jump on top of him and tickle him until he gave up. As the sun set over Saba's humble apartment, we'd take turns in his big, old-fashioned barber chair pretending we were cutting his hair. Then, after he got us all wired, my mother would yell at him and at us, and we'd have to go to bed. Sometimes my big sister, Ga, got to stay up late. She would sit in the kitchen with Saba trading stamps. He would sell her old, worthless Russian stamps for her stamp collection. She was sixteen and vulnerable. He was seventy and broke. He took the American money of his own granddaughter and went drinking with his sons.

Years later we found out how much the barber chair meant to my mother. While all her brothers were in school getting an education, she had to work at her father's barbershop cutting hair. He didn't see why girls needed an education. He was a mean, angry boss and wouldn't let her keep any of the money she made. When she was sixteen, she ran away from home for a few months, but he found her and dragged her back home. Every night she sat in the same corner of the barbershop at closing and cried by herself. No one ever came to save her, not even her own mother. I think Saba was the catalyst for my mother completing high school and then Marymount College at nearly fifty years old. Unfortunately, he had passed away years before. The day she graduated to a standing ovation, she told us that he still owed her money and that she was still pissed!

OCTOBER 10

It was freezing out this morning. I guess even California summer is really over. I went out to water the vegetables. We really lucked out with all these great vegetables. I'm now spoiled and don't think I can ever buy another tomato at the supermarket. Bill was outside doing tai chi. It is beautiful to watch. He tried teaching me but we fought too much. He would stand there, hands on his hips and say, "You just want to do things your way, while the masters have been doing this for several thousand years! Either do it right or don't waste my time." Then I would walk away in a silent huff. He gets annoyed with me because I'm so impatient. I hate him because he thinks he does everything right. Then we go inside, have tea and oatmeal, and act as if nothing happened.

Later I went out to pick some tomatoes, eggplants, and peppers to make ratatouille, and Bill was out there fiddling around with the hummingbird feeder. Of course we haven't seen a hummingbird yet. He cleaned the feeder out, filled it up again, and moved it into a sunnier corner where the seven neighborhood cats are less likely to chase birds.

It's nice to know he still has some hope to balance against all of our botanical cynicism.

OCTOBER 14

Last night I came home from a shoot in Los Angeles, drained. There are so many Hostess Twinkie motherfuckers in this business, and somehow they all seem to find me. All week the director yelled and yelled. First thing in the morning, he picked on the crew. Then, when the cast showed up on set, he put on a big, fake smile and turned into Mr. Nice Guy. It made us all want to throw up. Day three we had a big fight outside of his trailer. I threatened to quit if he didn't stop screaming at everyone around camera. He said he didn't give a damn what I did. I just love a supportive work environment!

The next morning, on the way to work, I found a radio program called *Nothing But the Blues*. They had an hour of the sisters singing "no-good-man" songs. It touched my soul and gave me strength. It was the only thing that got me out of the car and onto the set with Mr. Personality. Actually, the only reason I came back the next day was because James Taylor was coming to the set to visit the soundman at lunch and I wanted to get a picture with him.

When I got home from L.A., I put on *Luck of the Draw,* made a gardenia bubble bath, put on my sky blue mud mask, had a rocket beer, and soaked away in the candlelight. I really enjoy hiding from the world. I enjoy it so much that I'm on the edge of being a dark and dangerous hermit. I stayed soaking in my gardenia bath for an hour thinking about the past—about New York City. I closed my eyes and my memories became sepia-toned pictures. Except for the gladiolas. Gladiolas are Ma's favorite flower. She was a total sucker for gladiolas, and in exchange for them she would easily (if temporarily) forgive you your sins of the day. The florist on 86th Street always had giant red and yellow gladiolas. I don't remember ever wondering where those flowers actually came from throughout my entire childhood. I guess I just thought they grew in the flower shop. By junior high school we were baby-sitting full time and filled the house with flowers on any occasion that we could, knowing it would put us on Ma's good side. The walk to the flower shop was an education in itself. We learned what sexual harassment was way before it was an issue. Walking down the avenues we'd have doormen (who were there for security!) making kissing signs behind our backs and saying, "Nice ass." At fifteen years, we learned to walk fast and give them the finger. Then, all of a sudden, their whole attitude would change. They didn't want us anymore, because we weren't flattered, and they'd say, "You gotta big ass, anyway . . . and you're ugly, baby."

Every morning Ca would sleep through her snooze alarm. I would have to get out of bed and shake her. Then I would go back to sleep for twenty more minutes, pissed off. Then I'd wait for her at the elevator so we could walk to the bus stop together.

October

Most of the time I got too impatient and left her. She would take
the train to Bronx Science and I would take the Madison Avenue
bus up to Music and Art high school, getting the scenic tour of
Harlem on the way up to 135th Street. I would stare out the window in disbelief and then — guilt. At night we would baby-sit for
the most affluent New Yorkers on Park Avenue and the next
morning I would ride through burned-down buildings, gray,
filthy littered streets with half-clothed children and poor old
men sitting on the stoops of their homes with broken and barred
windows staring out hopelessly. I was filled with rage and wondered if President Nixon had ever visited here. I think every
person in America should be required to take this tour. Maybe
they'd start appreciating what they have and realize how much
poverty is still out there behind the blinders we put on to make
us feel safe.

Sometimes I still feel like a naive teenager and wonder how
we ever let this happen.

After school we would each have to practice the piano for an
hour. It was torture. Our teacher, Mrs. Aldendorf, smelled like
old ladies' skin cream and she was annoyingly eager. I would be
falling asleep to the ticking of the metronome, and she'd be there
ecstatically pulling out her gold stars. If you had performed the
piece perfectly, you'd get a star and be ready to move on to a new
piece. It took me weeks to get on to a new piece of music. I simply wasn't motivated. I just couldn't wait to get my lessons over
with so I could go mope in my room, listen to Neil Young, and
wonder why there was never any peace in our house.

Max fell head first into the bathtub and woke me from the
past! He's such a lunatic! I got out of the bath and put on Schu-
bert's 'Ave Maria' loud enough to hear outside. I put on Grandpa
Max's pajamas and went out into the cold, clear, starry night.
Maui and wet Max tiptoed behind me into the backyard. We sat
under the plum tree, curled up in blankets, and listened to those
violins over and over until we were so sad, and I cried for the
whole sorry world.

OCTOBER 18

It is absolutely freezing outside today, and I feel so lethargic. I walked around the driveway, took one look at my icy, miserable, nonblooming garden, and got depressed. All the summer blooms are gone. Everything is losing its color and its leaves. Winter is almost here and it's getting on my nerves.

Work is slow, the garden looks like hell, and it's almost time for the holidays.

Where can I run and hide?

I hate everything and everybody today.

No reason. No PMS.

Just feel like it.

Everything sucks. Especially this stupid garden journal.

OCTOBER 21

Yesterday is over, thank God. Today is a clear, crispy, sunny autumn day. I went to visit Gwyneth in Santa Cruz. We walked through the mustard fields along the railroad tracks and talked about men. We had theory after theory, and then a whooole *new* theory. We went on in our singsong way, analyzing men and women. Non-story after non-story, as we figured out the challenges of marriage and how to keep long-term relationships passionate. I guess if we had the answer to that we'd be rich. We walked for an hour or so past the barnyard animals. The goats spit at us as if they were disgusted with our conversation. They had an air of superiority. As the sun was setting, I showed her the first eight stances of tai chi that Bill had patiently taught me. Then we headed home arm in arm.

On the ride north from Santa Cruz, I stopped at Half Moon Bay. I went for a run along the water. It was early morning, and the beach was empty except for me and a Chinese fisherman. I started thinking about Ma, and immediately the tide rushed in and I got soaked. I was thinking about being sixteen and all the times I had to sneak food to Carol, hidden in the stairway. She was always mouthing off to Ma. Sometimes she was right and sometimes she was wrong. It didn't matter. She had even more pride than Ma and would scream back. There I was, the little goody-goody mediator, trying to make everyone get along. Ha! Fat chance! Ma would demand an apology, Ca would refuse, and then she would be locked out of the apartment. After I cleaned up the table, and Ma was watching TV, I would sneak food into the stairwell. Fluffy would come with me. He tiptoed out with me into the long, cold hallway. He was afraid of Ma too. That's why I loved him so much. We brought Ca dinner, reading material, and the key to the apartment so she could sneak in later when the coast was clear. I would leave Fluffy with her for company, then go back home and try to calm down Ma, who was usually hysterical by then. My mother has a vicious temper. I think she could scare even the biggest, bravest man and have him running for cover. She's big and tough on the outside, but on the inside she's filled with gushy love. So there I was comforting her each night. My father was on business trips forever, and then he wanted a divorce. They tried talking but were too angry to get anywhere. It's a shame when you get to the resentful and blaming stage. It's hard to move past that. This went on for years. My mother was in a lot of pain. Instead of letting us in, she pushed us away and blamed everyone else in the world except herself. This is a defense mechanism, I guess. She blamed my father for ruining her life and she blamed us for not being exclusively on her side.

OCTOBER 24

I went around and cut back a bunch of perennials this morning—the yarrow, salvia, liatris, pincushion, and wallflower. Even though they look totally dead, I still have trouble cutting them to the ground. I have this fear that they'll never come back. But they do! Next, I cut back and fertilized the geraniums on the deck. I also fertilized the camellias and the rhododendrons in the shade section. They don't bloom much. We call that section the biggest bust so far. Later on, I glanced at Martha Stewart's *Living* magazine. Barbara gave it to me so I could look at the pictures of Martha's garden and weep!

Is she for real or what?

OCTOBER 25

Well, it's Halloween again. I hate most holidays, and Halloween is still high on the hate list. We're invited to a party, but you have to dress up, so we're not going. In fact, we're going away for the weekend so we don't have to be around for all the brats. Ha ha. I don't think our five-year-old neighbor, Rebecca, will come around this year anyway since last year we gave out raisins and apples. When Ca and I were seven years old, we walked all over Manhattan collecting candy in ballet and tap dance costumes. Ma let us put on Sha's ballet tutu, pink shoes, wig, and her tap dance outfit. When Sha noticed they were missing, Ma said that *she* had been dressing up in them! Sha believed this until she saw the photos come back. Then she got pissed off at us, and at Ma for sneaking around behind her back. If my mom hadn't been so obsessed with taking pictures, we wouldn't have always been in so much trouble with Sha.

OCTOBER 27

This afternoon I went to my interview for the Master Gardener program. I don't know why I brought them a business card and resume. I'm so used to film-job interviews that it just seemed the normal thing to do. They probably thought I was weird. The three women in charge were sooo serious. I forgot how serious Horticulture is and I don't think they'll let me in their little clique. Since

I won't be able to be present for all the weekday afternoon classes, I got the impression that I wasn't a strong candidate. God, I'm so jealous of anyone who has time to get their Master Gardener Certificate. Some of us have to work for a living! Maybe they knew I was kissing up to them throughout the interview. I mean I was practically begging. I was going on and on about how I just love, love, love to garden. I think I lost them when I got a bit esoteric and went on about planting, abuse, growth, recovery, and self-knowledge.

I guess they didn't do drugs in the eighties.

OCTOBER 28

I spent a long time chopping up the dead tomato plants and putting them into the compost. I really got into it because I was mad at the world. I had just found out that Cecily's mother has been diagnosed with lung cancer. She has only a few months to live. Cecily's mother is beautiful. She is a painter and paints flowers. For some reason, I always thought that someone who paints such beautiful, magical landscapes couldn't get a horrible disease. I thought they might be protected by their art.

You'd have to meet Cecily to get the whole picture. She's somewhere between a debutante and a homegirl. When I first met her, she was driving around in a broken down, white 1963 Ford Falcon convertible, with a scarf tied around her head like Jackie Kennedy. She was living in the Mission District in San Francisco. Her car had no locks, no windows, and no heat, yet she spoke so properly and politely as if she were the Queen of England. The first time I came to her apartment, she had just successfully chased a rat out of the bathroom with a stick. I was very disturbed by this, but Gwyneth and Cecily were so nonchalant that I just casually laughed along with them. Gwyneth and I want to make a movie where every fifteen minutes you see Cecily in her car, wearing her Jackie O. scarf, driving by in the background. This non-story, mysterious character would be the subtle, hidden meaning of the entire film. Though I'm not sure what the hidden meaning is yet.

I'll be there to hold Cecily's hand. It hurts me so much to watch my girlfriends lose their mothers. I don't know how you survive without your mother. I feel like such a baby. Ma drives me crazy, but I don't see how I could possibly live without her.

OCTOBER 31

Today is the beginning of the Mexican holiday "Day of the Dead"; the day you go to the cemetery with tortillas and drinks to honor the dead. I just love that. Since one grandfather is buried in Florida and the other in Israel, I had my own little picnic under the plum tree, where we buried Ebb. Ebb was our favorite cat. He was hit by a car. Once we got over Ebb, we got Max from the Humane Society. Max gets on our nerves most of the time, but there are those times where I think he's a little magical. Like today, during my ritual with my dead grandfathers, he came over to the picnic table and dropped a dead lizard from his mouth, right in the middle of the plate of tortillas. I think he wanted to be part of the festivities.

November

NOVEMBER 2

Last night Bill brought in the mail. On the top was the Jackson and Perkins Rose Catalog! I went through it page by page, drooling and dreaming that one day I'd have perfect roses just like the pictures. I ordered four roses; Heaven, Bonica, Love Potion, and Happy Trails. They'll arrive bare root in January, and then I'll have to sneak them into the ground without Bill, the rose patrol, noticing. It's Sunday today, and we're having the first true rain of the season. We woke up at 7:00 A.M. and put on layers of sweaters and raingear to transplant. The rhododendrons in the front yard, left by the previous owners, were planted in the wrong place. Burned by the sun, they looked miserable. They grew into bushes but they never flowered. Today we attacked all three of them. We told them how lucky they were to be getting a second chance. Now they better do something with themselves and not be so lazy, like the cats. We dragged the bushes out of the ground and moved them to the shady and acidic soil under the two redwoods. We planted two oleanders in their place. One would think that oleanders would be simple because you see them all along the California freeways, but that's not the case around here. Last year's oleanders haven't put out one single flower. Figures.

As we were out there digging holes in the mud, dripping wet, all seven neighborhood cats came over to watch. We were surrounded by them. The two black cats on the red bench; Fatcat under the cherry tree; Psycho kitty and the mean, ugly one on the picnic table; and Maui and Max sitting closest to us. They all were very intrigued at having human beings outside in the rain with them. I kept whispering to them "This is our little secret," so they wouldn't tell their owners that two lunatics live next door. We were out in the rain for close to two hours and we didn't fight once! We must really be growing up. I don't miss fighting, but I wonder if there's a catch here. I look forward to us being in our eighties together. I'll still be sneaking in rosebushes. He'll still be finding them and saying I planted them too close.

Then I'll hit him with my cane and walk away in a huff.

NOVEMBER 5

I just got home from another shoot from hell. Who do these people think they are? They're certainly not brain surgeons or rocket scientists, even though they act like it. They're spending $45,000 a day on yet another P.O.S. (piece of shit) TV movie. The director was an arrogant idiot and the lead actor was psychotic. All morning he screamed in the middle of City Hall, "Where the fuck are my script pages? I want revisions *now*. Not five minutes ago. Not later. Not tomorrow. *Now.*" (Of course, the pages were personally handed to him yesterday. They were sitting in his trailer.) Two minutes later he's over by the camera, talking about the weather as if nothing had ever happened. This is what drives me crazy. If someone's going to be a jerk, they may as well stay one. That way you can thoroughly enjoy hating them.

The rest of the day he complained about his luxurious suite at the Majestic Hotel. I guess he couldn't see the twenty thousand homeless people when he looked down from his penthouse terrace. People like him used to really bother me, but this business is so full of them that I kind of expect it. If they're really horrible, and I can't stand it any longer, I say what my mother and Safta have passed down the generations to us, *"Shcee be tachad,"* and walk away. It means something like shove it up your ass, in Hebrew. If that doesn't help, spitting in their coffee on the last day will usually make me feel better.

I drove home in the rain with Bonnie Raitt blasting on the radio. Tears of exhaustion were streaming down my face. Just as I was belting it out at the top of my lungs, I got pulled over for speeding. Giving me a speeding ticket is ridiculous because I'm a goody-goody driver and most of my friends hate driving with me because I drive so slowly. Now I have to go traffic school with those people who aren't even funny. When I got home there was a message from Cecily about her mother's chemotherapy not going well.

Some days really suck.

NOVEMBER 14

Today is my parents' wedding anniversary. For years I called my mother to say "Congratulations," even years after they were divorced. This year I decided that it was sick and that I should finally get over it and stop living in the past, so I didn't call. I had a decent, uneventful day, and when I came home in the evening Ma called, sounding hurt and asked me if I'd forgotten. I said, "No, of course I didn't forget. I was just about to call you. Happy anniversary!"

NOVEMBER 15

It's been almost a year since Grandpa Max's death. I was thinking about him a lot today while I cleaned out the shed. He had been ill for months and was struggling along in a Miami hospital. When he died, it was a rude awakening for all of us. He had been the head of the family and the one who kept the family close. My sisters and I hadn't even dealt with anyone close to us dying. We were very lucky in that way. I always thought that Grandpa would be here forever and that my sisters and I would never have to grow up.

A few years ago, I asked Grandpa if I could have his dancing ballerina music box with the cigarettes inside. When we were kids, my sisters, my cousin Suzy, and I would sit around eating

Belgian chocolates and watching the ballerina dance. Then we'd all take a cigarette and pretend we were sophisticated ladies, puffing and discussing world affairs. The music box still brings back happy memories of the family together on holidays. Grandpa put it in a brown paper bag, threw in some Coffee Nips, and told me not to tell anyone that he gave it to me. It sits on my dresser today alongside the picture of Fluffy swimming in the fountain, outside the Metropolitan Museum.

Grandpa's funeral was small, and I thought it really didn't do him justice. I've never felt so sorry for my dad. He looked lost even though he tried to be strong in front of us. I spent the longest week of my life with Grandma Rose after the funeral. Every morning she would wake up crying. She went on and on about how she had nothing to live for. Then she'd look at me and hesitate as if she were coming back down to earth and say: "Did you eat breakfast? You're too skinny. You should eat." Talking about food seemed to keep her happy, so I brought up the subject a lot, since it makes me happy too. But she would slip back into her missing-Max-mode throughout the day. I didn't quite know what to say, since losing Bill would be absolutely devastating to me. How would I go on without my rocket scientist? Who would I argue with? I couldn't even imagine such a loss after spending fifty years together. And, of course, Grandma Rose was a totally dependent wife! She never learned how to drive, never had a paying job, and never really went anywhere without Max on her arm. When Grandma heard that my sisters and I had all purchased our houses with the money we earned ourselves, she couldn't quite get how that was humanly possible. Once we explained it to her, she liked the concept of your own paycheck and bragged about us to her friends at the poolhouse.

So I sat in that barley-smelling kitchen with poor Grandma Rose each morning, trying to find things for her to look forward to. The days dragged on and on. It was so damn humid and hot. I had no energy. The big event of the day was going for a walk. It took Grandma an hour to get ready for it, and it was over in fifteen minutes. Then I would slip into my own depression and she'd be in her depression and we'd be dripping with sweat and it felt like we were drowning in loneliness.

At night she would cry herself to sleep or I'd give her a sleeping pill. Each night I'd wake up at 3:00 A.M. in Grandpa's study, sweating in his pajamas. I'd turn on the light and examine all his gadgets, calculators, shoehorns, prayer books, and the "things to be done" on his religious desk calendar. I felt some part of him was in the room with me. I was thankful for the sun coming up each morning. The nights were so scary.

When I left Grandma Rose, she had progressed in her heartbreak recovery. The last day I was there, she got up the nerve to take the apartment complex bus all by herself to the market. There she was at the bus stop, feverishly waving her cane for the driver to stop. I was so proud of her.

At the airport in Miami, returning from the funeral, something happened that only happens in the movies. I was getting on the airplane back to wonderful San Francisco when a familiar voice called my name. I turned around and it was Arthur, the guy I thought I was madly in love with ten years ago. Of course, I looked like hell after mourning for a week in a disgusting, humid heat wave. Of course, he looked absolutely gorgeous! It's a long story, but the gist of it is that I was in love with him and he just kinda, sorta liked me. This went on for a year or two. I called him, we got together, he watched football, I wanted to talk, he watched hockey, I was pissed off, he watched baseball. I guess that about sums it up. So there we were on a two-hour flight sitting together and actually having a great time talking.

We talked about the past. He didn't remember much. That's how much I meant to him. Men! The night that he broke up with me, my mother and I walked around my block about twenty times, talking. That night she was more my best friend than my mother. She had her arm locked in mine and told me over and over how this would pass and I would get over him. And she was right.

(Do guys just forget that stuff? In all my single years, I never figured them out. The only thing I know that still stands true is the "three day rule." After a date with you, they won't call you for at least three days. Then, by the time you've cried yourself to sleep, called the operator to make sure your phone still works, called all your girlfriends to bash him, and then decided to totally hate his guts, he will finally call and you have to sound nice, cheery, and calm.)

So I told Arthur how great Bill is and how much we love each other; about how many different medical licenses Bill has and that he's an avid rock climber, nature photographer, horticulturist, triathlete, rocket scientist, and, that . . . he is dying to marry me. Arthur is now married to a rich, perfect blonde.

Figures.

When I got off the plane in Dallas for my layover, my mother was there with her camera aimed at Arthur and me. She was clicking away before I even introduced her to him. She said, "So this is the one." She just gave him one of her looks. She had never met him, but she knew the whole story. She told him he was forgiven, but to stay far away from me.

Then she took his picture and mumbled something under her breath in Russian.

NOVEMBER 16

Help! I'm turning into my mother. I walked around the garden staking up the few blooming plants and told them to stand up straight. Then I took pictures of them. Then I made Maui and Max pose on the red bench. That didn't work. Max pounced on Maui immediately. I'm trying to document each month in the garden so that I can remember what is supposed to bloom when and what is just remaining a bust and wasting my time. My mother and I are pretty obsessed with taking pictures and documenting events. We've had this contest going for years. She has pictures of herself with famous people, and then, when she talks about them, she calls them "my friend." For instance, "My friend Hillary" or "My old friend Sarah Vaughan died today. I can't speak." It cracks my sisters and me up. We get a kick out of Ma's important friends. I began competing with her recently, on the set and at political functions. The only difference is that I call everyone "My close, personal friend." Someday I'd like to put a photography book together called *My Mother's and My Own Close, Personal Friends*.

When Bill came home, I was organizing and dating the pictures of the plants. I had the *Western Garden Book* open and was highlighting information about each one. He looked at me, rolled his eyes, and said: "Babe, don't you think we've put enough effort into this yard and it still looks like a weed patch? We're better off using a scratch pad and a Ouija board."

He must have had a bad day.

NOVEMBER 17

I knew things were going a little too well. I'd been working a lot and still finding time to work out, see Bill, and have a life. Things were just peachy. Then I got a call this morning that my father had a heart attack. He was at work on an assignment in Puerto Rico. He was getting off the plane when he felt dizzy and started having chest pains. He made it to the hotel and called for help. A so-called doctor who only spoke Spanish showed up with a wheelchair and ran behind, pushing my father for six blocks to the hospital. After hours of medical deliberation and back and forth phone calls, my father is flying back to New York at the end of the week. There they will decide if he needs surgery.

I've been sick to my stomach today, pacing. It's been pouring rain. I was angry all day long. I was angry at my father for being a workaholic and for eating too much ice cream. I was angry about having childhood secrets. Even when my parents were legally separated, my father didn't want our mother to know that we had gone to lunch with him and his new companion. He said it would hurt Ma too much and then she would take it out on us. So we had to pretend we didn't see him with anyone else. Ga decided to stop seeing Daddy altogether because it was too convoluted. Sha and Ca didn't want Ma to suffer anymore, so they said that he was alone. They knew my mother would always believe we were on my father's side, plotting against her. But, not me! I told her EVERYTHING! Our stories never matched. How could the three of us have had the same dinner with the same father and two sisters not have seen another woman there? So Sha and Ca would be mad at me, and we would have countless, painful debates on what was the right thing to do. Without ever being asked, we were thrown into the boxing ring to help fight out our parent's difficult and drawn out divorce.

All this time I thought if I was open and honest with my mother, I'd be her best friend, her pet. Years later I finally learned that you couldn't win with my mother, so instead of hitting my head against the wall any longer, I moved three thousand miles away and now I miss her. That's what's great about life. No matter what you do, you're screwed.

Today, many years later, I can tell the truth. I can call my mother and tell her my father is about to get his his chest ripped open. No more secrets. I guess it's okay to tell ex-wives the bad news but not the good stuff. When people hate each other in a divorce, is this what they wish on each other? I hope I never know the feeling. I explained the surgery to her, how they take a vein out of his leg to put into his heart. I was half nauseated and half fascinated by this procedure. My mother kept *ts*king. She pleaded that she never wished this on him.

I went out to the garden in a daze and pampered every single flower, hoping that my father's Godiva-covered arteries would somehow feel my healing. When I came back in, there was a message from my mother. She had called my father to wish him good luck on his heart surgery. I almost fainted.

NOVEMBER 20

Today was Dad's heart surgery, for real. He'd been in the NYU Medical Center emergency room for five days. That had to be hell! Since we live in such a violent society, bigger emergencies kept shunting his procedure aside. Stabbing and gunshot victims passed by his side as he patiently waited to be chopped up. My poor dad. We tried to laugh on the phone and sound so cool about it all. Then I would hang up the phone and cry all over the geraniums. I couldn't concentrate at work and at the Safeway I was mad at all those stupid people going on with their lives, instead of stopping the world and worrying about my father. Sha called in the evening from New York and said that everything went well and that she saw Dad in intensive care. When Bill came home I was crying all over the five-page letter I had written to my dad apologizing for being pissed off at him for so many years and letting him know that I don't hate men anymore.

NOVEMBER 23

It was another rainy day today. I started out sad, thinking about my Dad's heart recovery, but now I feel optimistic and goofy because I just came back from a great double feature. *Priscilla: Queen of the Desert* and *Ed Wood*. Two strange movies! I've decided I'm going to be nauseatingly optimistic and happy, just like Ed Wood. I'm going to go around and speak in his singsong tone and get on everyone's nerves! Just like that!

I went straight to the garden to get a salad ready for dinner, and there were brand new radishes! Radishes are so easy to grow that even a New Yorker can do it. They should be the first vegetable grown by any beginner gardener. I listened to the message from my dad. He sounded so good. It's been almost a week since his open-heart surgery. He said to call him as soon as I got home because he had good news. I called him back right away. He said he was going to RETIRE. This may sound easy to you, but it's actually very difficult, since all of us in this family are obsessed with work.

I got off the phone and my head was spinning. I wasn't sure where I was going to fit a father in. He said he was coming out to visit next month. He won't be traveling all the time on business trips. No more Brazil, Germany, Argentina, and France. There'll be no more calls at strange hours with static on the line from foreign countries. No more excited calls from our favorite restaurant in Paris that has *pommes frites,* with mustard sauce to die for. He won't be calling to say, in his ecstatic Ed Wood tone, "I'm in Paris with Phillipe! We're having lunch at the Steakhouse!" He'll be at home, in crazy, cold New York City, retired, and we'll get together and do things. How did I get so lucky as to have a second chance at a close and honest relationship with my father? I'm going to work on this friendship because I know that it's a gift. I know he thinks it's a gift too, because he says he still reads my drippy letter a couple of times each day.

NOVEMBER 24

This is why I love my friend Barbara, in Colorado. She called me today to tell me that she hates people who say "You betcha!" Then I told her that I hate people who say "Have a good one!" Then we both agreed that we hate people who say "Happy as a clam!" I mean, are clams really happy? Has anyone ever stopped and asked them?

NOVEMBER 25

Thanksgiving is here. I'll be leaving for Texas tomorrow to visit Ma. The holidays continue to depress me. All I really want to do is sleep. I get so tired of hearing "Merry Christmas." It's so hypocritical in this greedy, selfish world we live in. All of a sudden everyone pretends they care. Where the hell are they the rest of the year?

The first year I met Bill, we spent Thanksgiving with his mom in San Francisco. Her house was so warm and cozy and it had a spectacular view of the city. Bill has five sisters and two brothers. I've never met a family quite like this. They're all extremely healthy and most of them are doctors or nurses. Before we pigged out at dinner, we were required to do a two-hour hike through Golden Gate Park with his mother, sixty-something, leading the way.

The thought of my family doing such a thing had me laughing to myself and tripping on rocks and twigs in the woods. No way would we leave the house with all that fattening food awaiting us. After our walk, when we finally sat down to eat our turkey, they all started calling each other by their childhood nicknames. They went crazy on me. In our family we simply have *Ga, Sha, Ca, and Ing.* Quick and simple. Bill's sisters' names are by far the strongest I've ever heard, and I now feel better to be part of this family because they're not so normal after all. From oldest to youngest they are: *Shoobie, Fizz, Burr, Mammer-Jammer, Wowie, Lampshade, Gump,* and my all-time favorite: *Cheryl-Kinka-Deryl-Sparrow-Marrow-Rum! . . . of the Third Armenian Calvary.*

The morning after Thanksgiving, at seven o'clock, we were all woken up by Bill's Mom to go to the eight o'clock aerobics class.

Is she for real?

You see, my family didn't know that people like this existed. Our holidays were spent at Uncle Bob and Aunt Ceil's house in Fieldston. We were the public school cousins who would always feel intimidated by the stone mansion on the pond. It took hours trying to find the right thing to wear so that Uncle Bob wouldn't make an embarrassing comment or Grandpa disapprove of your "hippie" outfit. The pressure was too much. The house was filled with tension before we left. By the time we were teenagers, we didn't want to go at all. The last place you want to be on earth is with your relatives. But of course, we always ended up having a great time and then we didn't want to leave. Now I give my mom and Aunt Ceil so much credit for trying to keep the family close and for being such graceful hostesses.

When we walked in the front door of Aunt Ceil's house, to a perfect Martha Stewart holiday dinner, Grandma and Grandpa were the first to greet us. They were always so excited to see us. Grandpa would be glowing, saying "Annie-Panny, Annie-Panny." It would break my heart. Aunt Ceil always had quite the spread. She had "colored" help in little white uniforms running around busily in the kitchen. My sisters and I spent time talking with them while we hid from Uncle Bob in the kitchen. He would find us and drag us off to see his latest antiques or toys or books. He would open up the bar and serve us Baileys on the rocks. He was brilliant, loving, and charming, but something about him scared us to death and kept us away.

Finally it was time to eat! The dining room had a shiny, sparkling chandelier and the long, glamorous table was perfectly set for twenty people. Ca and I would find out where our cute cousins Ron, Rick, and Peter were sitting and make sure we were right in the middle of them. They were in college and cool. We were in junior high, awkward, and weird, but we still wanted to flirt with them. Sha and Cousin Sue and her stupid little kick-dog, thought they were groovy because they were two years bigger than us, and they sat together. Ga would sit near cousins Art and Claude and discuss existentialism. Ma and Daddy would be near Grandma and Grandpa and all the other grown-ups.

Before we could begin eating, Grandpa would break in with a prayer and go off mumbling in Hebrew for twenty minutes. I couldn't look at Ca at this point because she would always make me laugh. It's hard to take religion seriously when you're twelve. (Actually, it's still hard for us.) At completion of prayer, if we were still awake, we stuffed ourselves to death and then we had dessert.

Then the grown-ups wandered into the mansion's livingroom and den for after-dinner drinks and conversation. Uncle Bob made us more drinks at his bar. When we were real young we would go play hide-and-seek in the basement. Uncle Bob's medical office was there and it was filled with scary examination tables and horrifying equipment. It felt haunted down there, as though it was filled with evil spirits. It made hide-and-seek a terrifying game and I couldn't wait to be found.

When I was a teenager and the games were over, I would go upstairs and take a nap so I wouldn't have to talk to anyone. I was too depressed in those years, and the only one I really enjoyed talking to was Cousin Ron, because he was miserable too. His room was in the attic where we could hide. He gave me my first Anne Tyler book, *Dinner at the Homesick Restaurant.* We shared secrets about our families. Some days we would try to figure out Uncle Bob. Other times we would discuss Ma. These were difficult relationships in our lives, and we were too simple to know how to deal with them. One minute they loved us so deeply and the next they turned into big, scary monsters. This kind of love was confusing and it would leave you wondering what you did wrong and shaking in fear until the storm blew over.

NOVEMBER 28

Yay! Thanksgiving is over. It is gray and cold in Dallas. It was another all-female holiday (Bill stayed with his perfect family, probably hiking Mt. Tamalpais). We haven't had Dad with us at Thanksgiving in more than ten years. I've grown accustomed to it, but this year I think we were all thinking about him and about his delicate mushy heart. We don't ask him who he spent the holiday with because we don't want to hear about his second wife and other family. I guess we're all still a bit in denial. We just want him for ourselves.

We had the most fun we've had in years with my mother last night. We ate an incredible turkey—the best stuffing in the world. No one has ever come close to my mom's stuffing. Then we taught Ma how to play Pictionary. It slipped our minds that she had been an art major in college and that she's the only one of us who can actually draw. She was amazing. She was out there at the dining room table painting away, winning points, sketching backdrops, whisking her pencil around in a mad artist's frenzy. We were laughing and screaming so much that Ca and I lost our voices. The last drawing Ma made was of a perfect, model-looking babe with a big chest, skinny waist, short skirt, and high heels. Then she kept pointing to her head. We screamed out every slutty word we could think of. We didn't get it. Ma looked at us as though we were retarded and said, "The answer is *blonde*. That threw us over into more hysterics. It must have been the sugar in the pies. We were absolute lunatics. I went to bed that night happy — happy to see Ma laughing again. She used to laugh all the time when we were young. She always laughed with us and smiled to us in the rearview mirror of the car. She would put on her 1960s orange-red lipstick and whisper "I love you" to each of us in the backseat. It always made me melt.

Ga and I woke up first and tiptoed around the house so we wouldn't wake up Ma. Her diabetes makes her moody and if she wakes up on the wrong side of the bed, it's all downhill after that. We put on Bob's old lumberjack layers and went outside with our gardening shears. We collected leaves for her compost pile, while she tried to explain 'Kant' (the philosopher) to me. I mean the guy must've been on drugs. Could he write one sentence that you didn't have to read ten times to comprehend. Is that too much to ask of the genius? When we came back in the Queen Bee was awake.

Ga, in a perfect Ed Wood tone, said, "Good Morning, How d' you sleep?"

Ma gave her a dirty look and said, "Why does she always talk to me when I'm trying to think?"

And so the games began.

Ma was bashing Ga, and I, of course, came in to defend my sister with a Ph.D. from being stepped on in her own home, and the whole world exploded. You see, my mother will be mean to whomever lives closest to her and right now that's Ga. We've all had our chance. Ma and I fought every week when I lived three blocks away from her in New York, but now that I live far away, I'm a wonderful daughter and she misses me. That's the trick. Some people push you away from them and you just gotta get up and go!

We sat down to have breakfast. I was looking at my mother, thinking how beautiful she still is, until she turned to me and told me it was rude to stare! Things calmed down slowly. Ca had tea with honey and, unfortunately for the rest of us, her voice came back. She went on and on about Stacey-Shmacey, Beth, Donna, Scott, and the rest of her soap opera life in San Diego. I was exhausted halfway through the first chapter of the story. Do her stories ever end? I was thinking about meals we had as a family in the past. When we were growing up, family meals usually meant Ca telling long, laborious, detailed stories about her and her girlfriends, and then we would all fight. The fight would begin because Ma wanted the window wide open and the rest of us were absolutely freezing. She needed air. Daddy would come to dinner with a down jacket, gloves, and a ski hat to make a point. Sooner or later, someone would say the wrong thing and there would be a war at the table. I don't know quite how this happened, but somehow everyone would escape and I'd be stuck clearing the table and washing the dishes and, yes, comforting Ma.

Later that day, Ga and Ma took me to the airport. An unfortunate United Airlines pilot was standing in the right place at the wrong time and was handed Ma's Instamatic and directed by the Queen Bee on how to shoot the family portrait, with the big, ugly parking structure behind us. He suggested a different background, and Ma yelled at him to mind his own business.

Can't he tell she bites?

Get a clue, buddy.

In a private moment, Ga told me she had been offered a teaching position at a school in Illinois. She was considering taking it and asked if we could move Ma to San Diego, near Ca. Now this is funny. Ca moved away from us all years ago in an effort to escape from the looney bin, and now she would have Ma in her backyard! I hugged and kissed my mother at the gate. I always cry deeply when I say goodbye to her. Walking down the platform to the plane I kept turning back and she was still standing there watching me. Why do they do that?

It only makes it hurt more.

December

December

DECEMBER 3

This morning Bill and I couldn't sleep. We were both wide awake at 4:45. I was so happy that he was up. I hate being an insomniac alone. We tossed and turned for a while and then decided to get out of bed. We dressed up in big sweaters, made spice tea, and sat on the red bench. Of course, Maui and Max had to be in the cool clique and followed us outside, suspiciously. We took an old, rusty, half-broken flashlight and did a nature walk. The azaleas and the camellias have tiny buds on them. The purple salvia and the Mexican sage are still blooming profusely with peppy, little, blue and yellow flowers, so they get bonus points. All of the mini-roses are blooming, and our favorite fight-provoking plant, the potato vines, are bursting with white blossoms. The most exciting thing is that lots of stems of bulbs are shooting up. It'll be months till they bloom, but it's still sort of amazing. We have a bit of hope now, but it could just turn out to be another bust.

At 5:30 A.M. we got into the jeep and drove up to our viewing spot on the top of the hill overlooking Petaluma. The sun was just coming up, and it was freezing, but we were content. We walked around at the top of the hill and watched a red tail hawk fly over us collecting stuffing for its nest. I watched Bill watching the hawk and all I could think about was that it's only twenty days left till New Year's, the proposal day. That woke me up a bit. Next we watched the deer family cross the road and run up into the hills, with the mom glaring back at us every couple of feet. I wanted to run with them. The thought of going to work tomorrow made me so depressed. I just wanted to stay out on our hill and watch the wild kingdom with Bill, my rocket scientist.

DECEMBER 6

This evening I was watching CNN, and there he was, Newt. I can't stand to hear his voice or see his face. He disturbed me so much that I ran out of the house and into the garden, gasping for air. I know I hide from the real world in my garden, but sometimes I find the world so unacceptable that the only thing left to do is to pretend it doesn't exist. Christmas holidays are just about to hit. Some years it feels okay and some years it just feels greedy and chaotic; buying things that no one needs and getting all stressed out about it. Bill will get me some new books, and I'm not sure what I'll get him yet. We'll donate some time and money. That way we'll feel that someone who really needs gifts will get them.

Besides that, I basically can't stand December.

DECEMBER 10

Today I have the flu and I'm so miserable. I just want to be out in the garden, but it's too cold outside and I can't even get out of bed. I just finished another job with a fat, alcoholic, abusive director. I swear, I attract them. The last day something happened to me that made me really wonder, once again, how people can be so cold and heartless. I had been feeling flu symptoms coming on and kept pumping vitamins in, but it was too late. I was basically a sick mess on the set. I kept working because I knew there was only a day or two left to the shoot. At lunchtime I felt really horrible and basically lost it. I went sobbing into the women's bathroom. There I was, lying on the floor with my script notes and walkie-talkie all thrown around the bathroom floor, hysterically crying in pain. Every part of my body was cold, and I was shivering. So, I'm in this state of hysteria, and the producer's young, blond wife (with a made-up job title) comes in and basically ignores me and goes into one of the stalls. She nonchalantly asks, "Annie, what's wrong?"

I whimper, "I . . . *sniffle-sniffle* have . . . *sob-sob* the flu."

In her cold, I-could-care-less, I-don't-have-time-for-peons tone, she says, "Oh . . . hope you feel better," flushes the toilet, and walks out.

For a moment I was in shock, then the door opened and Gwyneth, my little angel, came in to save me. She brought me hot water and lemon. I told her the story, and all of a sudden it was the funniest thing in the whole world. We both laughed, and then I started crying again. We couldn't figure out exactly what makes people like that. I decided the only revenge was to pretend I was the blonde's best friend and go breathe my sick germs all over her for the rest of the job. I executed this plan for the entire twelve-hour day. My goal was to be as close to her as possible. I didn't care about the real job anymore. I had a goal. My aim was to find her and give her my germs. Coughing, breathing, honking, and wiping—whatever it took.

Every few hours Gwyneth and I would meet behind the trailers and spin. We always spin (a non-graceful pirouette while tossing walkie-talkies in the air) when we've accomplished any small, private, and trivial goal that we have set out for ourselves. It makes us feel superior, and we obviously need that.

DECEMBER 14

It was the first sunny day in weeks. I did a full garden walk with Maui, Max, and Fatcat. We did some much needed weeding in the rose garden. It's been raining on and off all month, and the weeds are back even stronger. I got into my hostile weed-pulling zone. If I think about the time I worked with James Woods, I can weed the entire rose garden spotless in record time. All I have to do is think about his malicious temper tantrums each day on the set. The crew would have to sit around for twenty minutes just waiting for him to shut up. One day during a rehearsal, he slammed an old, broken door and "a shard of wood," as he called it, flew into his eye. The producers must've mistaken me for someone who cared and I was elected to travel in the back-seat with James and LJ, the set paramedic, to the emergency room. James sat between us and each time that he'd lean down to cover his eye, LJ and I would do a quiet high five over his head and make faces to each other. When James would look up, LJ and I would look out the passenger windows trying not to look at each other and contain our laughter. We had to listen to James go on and on about his eye. It was torture. Of course, his eye was fine and I thought that he got what he deserved. Usually I'm not such a cold and inhumane person, but for that fifteen-minute ride to the hospital, I just couldn't wipe the smirk off my face no matter what. I was so pleased with God that day.

I got bored with weeding quickly and went over to the veg-etable garden and pulled out the last tomato bush. We had the last good tomatoes a few days ago. I chopped up the bushes and put them in the compost. I was in a neurotic chopping, cleaning, and compost organizing frenzy when Daddy called. I heard his voice on the answering machine and ran inside to the kitchen. He sounds so good. We talk a couple of times a week now. He's my newest friend. We talk investments, low-fat dinners, my lat-est job, and how much he misses coffee Häagen-Dazs. I tell him there are better vices in life, but I can't really think of any at the moment. He said he wants to meet Bill and me at the Grand Canyon in January. His doctor says it's okay for him to travel. I can't believe it. I can't believe all this good stuff is happening. I can't wait to hug him and tell him how happy I am to have him back in my life, in person, at the Grand Canyon. I went back out into the damp, cold, miserable garden and continued compost-ing. I was thinking about my father. When we were kids, we woke up many times to the sound of my parents fighting. Because I was the lightest sleeper I would be the first awake. I would sneak out into the hall and huddle in a dark corner to eavesdrop. My mother was usually the one doing all the talking. Other times they would simply slam doors, and then my father would leave. I would cry. I hated my mother for making him leave. I hated my father for leaving. I would try to wake up Ca, but she was so stubborn, even in her sleep, that she would just growl and push me away. So I would sit up on my bed, wondering if my father would ever return, until I finally fell asleep. In the morning, there he was. He would always come back to us somewhere in the middle of the night, just like magic. Every Saturday morning, we would stand on line next to my parents' bed, which looked to us like a giant's bed. My father would take us one at a time, hold us tight in his arms, and roll us across that big river of a bed, back and forth, as we lay screaming and laughing for more. We did this over and over, until my father was dizzy. Then we all went into the kitchen to make breakfast and watch him try to flip an omelet. He would put on a show for us and we ate up every drop of it. We would sit on the floor, using the big, plastic, sixties-olive-green chairs as our table, and watch cartoons. When we were done, my father would scrub our hands in warm, soapy water with his big, strong grown-up hands and we would look up at him, in love.

Monday morning he would leave again on another business trip.

DECEMBER 16

I attacked the rose garden again today, weeding till my arms were sore. I was mad at Bill so it was easy to do. We fought about money last night and about babies, work, life, and why there was oil leaking from my Jeep. I left. I always want to be the one to leave first.

I went to my favorite bookstore. They closed at midnight. When I returned home Bill wasn't there, and that really got to me. I wanted to be the latest one home! He came in a few minutes after me. He had been at the used bookstore two blocks away. We talked a little; it helped some, but there's still distance between us. Maybe we're both backing out of the possible marriage proposal only two weeks away. I bet that's it. We're both simply scared to death.

DECEMBER 18

It was cold and foggy all day in that boring, dreary garden. I can't wait till winter is over and life is blooming again out there. Hanukkah is over and Christmas is almost here. I'm slightly excited about it. I'm excited about spending time alone with Bill, even though I hate his guts today. We've both been working late these past few weeks and haven't had much time for each other. I've been traveling and it always takes both of us a few days to adjust to my being back. I don't see how a relationship can last when someone travels all the time. Some distance is good, but too much is dangerous.

DECEMBER 21

Today is Grandma's ninetieth birthday!
Simply amazing that anyone can stand to live that long.
Go, girl!

DECEMBER 22

Ro called today from Boston. We speak only a couple of times a year these days, and it always leaves me feeling a bit melancholy. Ten years ago we were single and waitressing at Christopher's in Cambridge, Massachusetts. Our daytime life consisted of going to the Beach in my Dad's old beat-up 1969 Cutlass. Our summer nights were filled with drugs, musicians, Baileys, and starving ourselves; and 90 percent of our conversations were about guys. What a waste of time. It's not like we ever figured them out. I was in love with Jim and she was in love with Billy. We were much better than them, but at the time, we had no self-esteem and didn't know how good we were.

When we weren't crying over Billy and Jim we were in court trying to collect ten years of child support for Ro's two daughters from her ex-husband. Nicole was just entering high school at the time and was basically miserable. I could relate to her because I was pissed off in those years too, so I became her confidante. She calmly confessed to me that she smoked pot and drank beer with her friends, and then, when Ro would come home from a hard day's work, Nicole would run around the house screaming, "I HATE YOU, I HATE E—VE—RY—THING." This went on for twenty minutes every night. I think this was the time in my life when I decided I didn't want to be a mom, because I need so much more recognition and appreciation than teenagers are capable of. Nicole was basically filled with anger and pissed off at the world because her parents hated each other. I don't know where the ex-husband disappeared to for years, but he's come around lately to befriend Nicole and Kristen. I guess it can't hurt if he shows them love, but where the hell was he when they needed him? And fork over the child support first, buddy.

Those few years of heartbreak, being broke, dancing, bringing up Ro's daughters, pretending we were flower arrangers at the Hyatt, running on the Charles River, buying lobster with our tip change, pushing my old Cutlass to start it, dieting and then bingeing on ice cream, watching poor Ro be so generous to the world, and lying on the beach analyzing mother-daughter relationships will always be on the top ten list of my life's most meaningful times.

DECEMBER 23

Elissa had a great Christmas party last night. She looked like a doll in her purple velvet dress. I gave her a Jackson & Perkins magenta rose tree for their backyard. Her son David got a fleece cap with side flaps that says ALPINE ADVENTURE. I told him true rock climbers, like Bill, wear hats like that, so that he would wear the thing. Big mistake. He spent the rest of the night following Bill around, asking when we were going to take him mountain climbing and why we couldn't go tomorrow morning.

Gwyneth, Cecily, Elissa, Ellen, Pucci, Cat, and I sat in the livingroom near the warm fireplace and amazing Christmas tree making New Year's resolutions. At some point in my life, I've fallen in love with every one of my closest girlfriends. It felt like I was twelve years old again and had just made a brand-new friend. The beginning of my friendships with each of them has been magical, passionate, exciting, filled with simple liking and true love. We've held hands. We hug all the time. We dance wildly. We laugh. We pick each other up and twirl one another in the air. Most of all, we listen and understand.

When we arrived home at midnight, there was a message that Cecily's mother had died. Her lung cancer had spread, and she went peacefully.

DECEMBER 24

It's Christmas Eve. We spent the day outside freezing in the garden. The only thing blooming on the side of the house is rosemary. Thank God for rosemary. Here it is freezing and gray outdoors, and this simple, trouble-free herb is blooming. Tomorrow I'll make rosemary-flavored vinegar to give to Mary Sheilds. She's Bill's favorite patient. She's eighty-one years old and she walks into Bill's office once a month saying, *"Doc, I fell on my ass again. . . ."* We transferred the four Breath of Heaven bushes to the backyard. They were being crushed by the wallflowers and had no room to grow. A true master gardener would have removed them months ago, but we've been too busy being workaholics. I guess we're basically lousy parents. Which reminds me, we've been out of cat food for two days and I haven't done a thing about it.

While we were digging holes in the ground and arguing about

placement of the plants, Rebecca, the kid next door, came over with a Christmas present for us. She brought over a gardening cap that said: SO MANY WEEDS, SO LITTLE TIME. She gave Bill five packages of seeds—arugula, endive, red peppers, red calabash tomato, and lemon cucumbers. This may seem like a simple gift to some people, but to us they're like gold, frankincense and myrrh. Seeds give us new faith. It's a codependency kind of thing we have with the garden. Just when we're about to give up on the garden, we're swept back in with the hope that things will get better.

DECEMBER 25

Yesterday evening we drove out to Point Reyes at sunset. It was Christmas Eve, and the town was lit up like in a fairytale. We walked around the local nursery to make sure nothing was blooming there so we could feel better about ourselves. We took a picture under a decorated, shiny, gold-laced tree. Then we walked along my private, secret beach as the sun was setting. It was cold and windy but there we were, arm in arm, laughing and singing along the water's edge. We stopped to examine all the jellyfish. I wanted to see their mouths, but we couldn't find anything that looked remotely mouthlike.

I showed Bill my log, the one I lean against in the summer when I go out there to hide from the world; to read and to write; to worship the sand, the ocean, the hills, the blue sky; and, of course, to be shallow by getting a bitching tan. As we were holding on tight, pushing through a sandstorm, I apologized to Bill for fighting with him a lot last week. The holidays bring up so many painful feelings of loneliness and depression in me. I want to cry for the whole human race and, selfishly, for myself. I wonder why my life sucks, but then I see other people's lives that are worse and feel guilty for not being thankful for having such an incredibly fantastic life, and it goes on and on. None of this fazes

Bill. He just acts like it's normal. Is it? He tells me how much he loves me. Will he ask me to marry him on New Year's Day? If he doesn't, will I ask him? These thoughts were racing through my mind as I covered my eyes against the sand blowing in my face.

On the way back to the car, it was dark, and we couldn't see the jellyfish, but we felt and heard them squishing under our feet as we accidentally stepped on their heads. We finally made it back to the old cozy, heated Jeep. All I could think of was my mother yelling at Bill. If she could see this deserted parking lot, pitch dark, on a cold and windy night, she'd never forgive him for taking me to such godforsaken places.

We put on old Etta James and drove the backroads to Petaluma. The town was sparkling. We walked along D Street admiring the Christmas lights twinkling across the historical mansions. We dreamed about the day we would live in one of them. Ha! Then we got depressed about the reality of that ever happening. Rich kids will inherit those houses and become right wing conservatives who want to overpopulate the world, but don't want any part of the food or healthcare costs, although they are willing to spend billions and billions to build more prisons and a nuclear shield around America to make us feel safe at home. And we'll still be in our backyard trying to get a rosebush to bloom. Not that that pisses me off or anything.

We had a fancy dinner in town. Half a glass of merlot and half a glass of champagne and I was even more madly in love with Bill. I just wanted to kiss him in between every bite. We got home late, but our neighbor New York Mike was still blasting Christmas music from his front porch. Jose Feliciano was singing "Feliz Navidad" as we pulled into our driveway, passing the fake deer with disco Christmas lights across the street. Fatcat and the real, live, big, brown pig were sitting on the front porch of the other neighbor's house across from ours. There was a Christmas card on the door from our friend Mooney. It said, "Happy Holidays to our favorite white trash couple."

Is that what we've become?

DECEMBER 27

Yay, the holidays are almost over! Bill and I exchanged books. I got something by Anne Lamott and he got a book about compost. Bill got a big red wagon and green plastic, spiked sandals from his brother-in-law Bobby. They're for aerating the lawn. I hope he doesn't plan to really wear them. The most surprising gift was my very own pair of E.B.'s, (rock climbing shoes) from Bill! What the hell was he thinking? Doesn't he get it? Hello? I'm from Manhattan. I don't climb up the face of a rock, hanging from a stupid rope. I was wondering when the day would come when he would want me to go climbing with him. He said it would change my attitude.

What's wrong with my attitude?

Bill is an exceptional climber. He's been climbing the highest peaks in the U.S. with his best friend John, since they graduated from high school. Almost every morning in their Jesuit-run ninth grade class, John, Bill, and their friend Puffa (who once fell out of his chair in the middle of a Theology test passed out on quaaludes) would get the class singing Happy Birthday to nerdy, dweeby Fred Synk. This is the kind of guy John is. He and Bill formed a climbing group called S.H.I.T. (Some Hot Intuitive Thoughts) Mountaineering. Bill calls John "Mr. Louie." It has to do with some dumb climbing story from twenty years ago, about a "lost fingerbook." You had to be there and had to be stoned. Whenever they're together, they regress back to useless, jobless, carefree rock climbers, and it gets on my nerves. Anyway, here I am with my own pair of E.B.'s, expected to climb with the best. All the years of attitude and abuse that I've thrown back into Mr. Louie's face are now going to haunt me. I'll be at his mercy on the rock and have to beg him to be patient and kind to me. If I wimp out of this, Bill will be disappointed with me. I'll never hear the end of it from Mr. Louie. He'll say that I always say *"women can do anything men can do,"* so why don't I prove it?

(God, sometimes I should just learn to keep my mouth shut.)

I told Bill the shoes were a very nice present and thank you.

However, I'm actually scared to death I'm not one of those women I was talking about in my previous generalizations about the sexes. He told me we'd go to the mountains in March, that he loves me, and that he knows I can do it.

My mother's not going to be pleased with this gift, and Bill is sure to lose his few brownie points.

DECEMBER 29

It's almost New Year's Eve, possibly the saddest night of the year unless you're superficial or drunk. Actually, I'm a little bit happy because we're going to the Grand Canyon! Five days of vacation with Bill, and the best part is that Daddy is meeting us for the last two days. I can't believe how well he's doing in his recovery. My father has traveled all around the world (well, maybe not everywhere). But he's never been to the Grand Canyon and neither have I. I can't wait. He sounded so peppy today on the telephone. He's planning to go to Italy in the spring and to Thailand in the summer. He certainly got into that retirement mode fast. I can't even imagine him relaxing and not wearing a suit. He was always one of those guys who wore dress slacks (*slacks* is his word, not mine,) and had a pen in his shirt pocket at all times, even on the weekends. I was always proud to introduce him to my friends. He would shake their hands and, in his low, fatherly tone, say, *"Hello, I'm Annie's dad."* Like he was president of the United States, which I always thought he should be. All my girlfriends loved him because he shared his knowledge of delicious ethnic foods, travel, politics, business, history, and the New York Stock Exchange with them. It's quite different from introducing my mother. She's just as entertaining and charming, but you never really know what you're going to get with her. It could either be, " 'You're single? You're too beautiful. What's wrong with all these shmata guys? Are they blind?" Or (big sigh), "Enough with all these friends. I'm exhausted. What's your name again? Oh, that's nice . . . Could you get me a glass of water? Oy, I can't breathe. . . . What's that shmata on your head? . . . Enough, I'd like to be alone with my daughter. Don't you have any manners?"

DECEMBER 30

Elissa and I went shopping today for after-Christmas sales. We thought it would be fun. Well, it wasn't. After twenty minutes I wanted to go home. Sometimes the thought of shopping is much more fun than the real thing. (Except for the one time years ago when Ca and I shopped for five hours straight and ended up on the dressing room floor of some cheap shit store laughing deliriously, in big, bright, tacky prom gowns and high heels.) Anyway, the afternoon turned out to be a success. Besides spending a few hours alone with Elissa, without her guy and kid, we found great pink flannel Barbie pajamas. I know Barbie is part of the problem of our generation's self-esteem but I had to get those pajamas.

When Sha was old enough to go to school, Ca and I would pull out her Barbie Dream House and play with her dolls. She was quite possessive back then, and we knew we'd be dead if she ever found out. One day we slipped. She found Barbie's red evening gown on Ca's bed. She screamed and cried and kicked until my mother finally said, "I've been playing with your dolls. I bought them and I can play with them." Sha believed her, and life went on as usual for a couple more years, until the day she found Ma showing Aunt Ceil a photograph of Ca and me grinning, surrounded by Sha's Barbie Playhouse, Ken, Midge, Skipper, and a plethora of their accessories. Boy, was she angry. She couldn't believe we all were sneaking around behind her back. I think I was hiding under my bed during the negotiation process. Basically, Sha was given the choice to share her dolls with us or my mother would throw the Barbies away forever. So poor Sha was forced to share with her two geeky little sisters with no front teeth.

January

JANUARY 1

Today is January 1. We spent the day cross-country skiing at the San Francisco Peaks, outside of Flagstaff, Arizona. We had a quiet New Year's Eve—dinner in town and then a long walk as the snow fell gently on us. I missed my sisters, and the tree at Rockefeller Center. I wondered if my mother was alone. I wondered what it would be like to see my father at the Grand Canyon, after they had ripped his chest open with an ax—well, kind of— and told him to stop eating food that tasted good.

We skied almost ten miles. There were great hills to torture yourself climbing and then come screaming down out of control. Bill, the triathlete, never tires, so we went on and on and on. The only thing that kept me going was counting to myself how many calories I was burning with every push and glide. Almost seven years ago, when I first went cross-country skiing with Bill, I hated it and I hated him even more. I had finally left New York. I had been in California for only one month before Mr. Adventure took me skiing in the Sierras, in the middle of a blizzard— as if this was normal. His best friend, Mr. Louie, was there with his wife, Pucci. They were having fun and I hated them all. During the six hours of snow captivity I kept thinking about the Indian cab driver I had the last night in New York on the way to Kennedy Airport. He was playing chimey tribal music and spoke very broken English except when it came to dollar amounts. He was speeding and beeping across the 59th Street bridge and singing loudly, like he couldn't care less that I was in the backseat. I was so happy to be getting the hell out of the big city. That is, until I went to the mountains with Bill. Trying to look graceful and getting off my butt at the same time, with-out sliding down the hill into another face plant, I realized that I had made a big mistake. I hated everything Bill enjoyed doing and I promised myself that if I made it out of this blizzard alive, I was going to dump him big time. Driving home in the car, I made him listen to Joan Armatrading's "Me, Myself, and I" over and over and told him I wasn't interested in a long-term relationship.

Love sure makes you do silly things. Today on top of the San Francisco Peaks, Bill asked me to marry him. In my very own dysfunctional style, I looked at him like he was out of his mind and asked him, "Why would you want to ruin a good thing?" He said, "Because, I truly love you." I felt that was a sufficient reply and I said, "Yes." I was happy at that moment, but the rest of the day I had a stomachache and felt like I was going to throw up. I kept telling myself it was the altitude, but part of me knew I was simply scared to death of marriage and inside of me there was an emotional volcano ready to erupt. I felt like my whole life was ending. I mean, if you're going to be a *husband* or a *wife*, you have to act like a responsible adult. Although, of course, that's not true. I know a lot of immature idiots who are married. Why is it so hard for some of us to grow up while others just seem to jump right in? Why am I holding on so tightly to my childhood when I thought it wasn't so perfect in the first place? Here it is, the first day of the New Year and I'm already freaking out.

We drove back to our 49er Room (the only inn available has sport's team rooms. Is that my luck or what? I hate football). I did what I always do. I called my mother. I told her we were planning to get married in September. She said congratulations and asked if there would be a rabbi. I said we could talk about it later. She said, "Fine," and went on to tell me who was on *60 Minutes*. I got off the phone in sort of a bad mood but didn't give in to it yet. I decided to call all of my sisters. All three of them sounded busy and, well, la-de-da about our engagement. They didn't get all excited about it like I wanted them to. I got off the phone and cried all over the stupid Joe Montana pillowcase. Bill took me in his arms and we talked. He said it's sort of anticlimactic since we've been together for nearly seven years. We talked about what marriage means to my sisters and me. It means fighting, leaving, and broken promises. It also means that our sisterhood is broken up and we might have to change and grow up.

I hate that.

I put on my Barbie pajamas and told Bill that I never want to be referred to as his *wife*. I hate that word. Why couldn't they come up with a better word? Then I fell asleep on the tacky Ronnie Lott comforter thinking about me being a *bride*. . . . Ha!

Now *that* is funny.

JANUARY 3

Daddy arrived today! He looks really healthy. It is just amazing that he can be doing so well after heart surgery. We picked him up and drove to our favorite restaurant in Flagstaff, "Macy's." Dad knew he was really out of New York City when we passed the road sign, ADOPT A HIGHWAY: WANITA WIGGINS, ASTROLOGER. We had a huge breakfast at the café. My father used to always order eggs for breakfast, but these days he's ordering oatmeal. He made me so proud. Celina, his wife, says he has tendencies to cheat and use cream in his coffee, or other such horrors, if no one is around, so we watched him like hawks at all times.

Bill told him about our wedding plans, and Daddy was excited about it. This meant so much to me. He's back in my life now as a friend and he wants to plan the whole wedding with me. This is just too good to be true. (Either he really, really loves me or he's just a retired workaholic and needs to be doing "a project" instead of relaxing.) Anyway, we sat around for hours having "a coffee" as Grandpa used to say and now Daddy says. We came up with all sorts of wedding ideas. We were thrilled to finally have a happy occasion to bring the family together. Dad will come out in March and we'll find the place and set the details. After hours of reminiscing and making future wedding plans, we finally drove to the south rim of the Grand Canyon.

It was a crispy clear, outstanding day. We walked around the flat area for about half an hour. Then Bill and I waved goodbye to Daddy as if we were going to another planet and hiked into the canyon. We walked for four hours in the beautiful canyon below. I'm sure Daddy found the coffeeshop and I'm sure he had real cream in his coffee. As usual, Mr. Adventure took me on the steepest hike of the entire Grand Canyon. My legs were getting sore, but it sure was pretty and I took a lot of pictures. We laughed about Bill's mom and how she labels and dates each and every one of her photographs on the back side. She has hundreds of photos, all labeled. It's amazing. She highlights her maps too! I thought that was really crazy until I started doing it, and now, of course, I think it's a brilliant idea. By the time we made it back up and out of the canyon, the warm sun was gone and it was freezing out, but there was my dad at the rim, taking pictures of me huffing and puffing my way up. I was far behind Bill, who was hardly breathing out loud at all.

I tell you, sometimes he makes me sick.

There are moments in your life that time can never erase. This was one of them. Looking up the Grand Canyon from a couple hundred feet below and seeing my father waving and taking pictures of us. It reminded me of the time he bought me my first camera when I was sixteen years old. We went to 47th Street together and picked out an old Canon. He taught me how to shoot with it. Then we found a used enlarger. We set up a darkroom in the bathroom, and he taught me how to develop black and white photographs. I would spend hours in there by myself. I took pictures of our dogs, of Ca putting on makeup with her best friend, Suzy, of Sha on her bike in Central Park, of Ga when she was a New York City taxi driver, of my mother on the terrace surrounded by our nice plants that we later admitted were pot, of my father walking to the subway, of Neil Young outside of Tiffany's, and of me playing Frisbee in the park with my sisters. I even took a few family portraits. As the images slowly materialized within the chemical trays, the emerging eyes and faces told the story of a family falling apart. When my parents finally divorced, and my mother had to move out of our apartment building, the box of photographs was lost and never found again.

JANUARY 4

The next morning we all got up early for breakfast at Macy's before we had to get on the road. It was our last day with Daddy. I was getting sad about that already. We got to the café and I made sure we sat at the same table so that it could be "Daddy's table" forever. We ate fast because the Fiddler family was just about to perform. They looked like the Von Trapps on LSD, and Bill and I didn't think we could keep a straight face during their performance. On our way out the door we passed the Leashman, a guy with a fluorescent leash around his neck.

I don't get it either.

We made Dad take a walk and get some exercise like he's supposed to, but he came up with all kinds of excuses — *'It's too cold'* and *'After my nap'* and *'Let's have a coffee first!'* I doubt we lifted his heart rate before he was ready for a coffee break, so we moved on and drove the magical, winding road to Sedona. The sun was peeking out through the flying saucer clouds over the vibrant red hills. The minute we arrived in Sedona, it started snowing enormous snowflakes. There went Dad's exercise. He found the nearest coffeeshop and we sat and had more tea and toast. Bill read the sports page while Dad told me about the cruise he went on with Celina last year; there was a fire on board and everyone had to escape on lifeboats. He was one of the few people that wasn't all freaked out, because he had escaped from the Nazis during World War II on a ship bound for Cuba. Nothing would ever again frighten him as much as that. Then he told me about being elected national president of Machal, an organization of American and Canadian veterans of the Israeli war of independence, which led to the creation of a homeland for the survivors of the Holocaust. (See I told you he can't relax. The day he retired, he became president of an honorable and prominent club.) I can just imagine these war heroes. They probably meet in restaurants with all their old pictures and letters and tell the same war stories over and over. And then they argue with each other about a specific date or name and no one can speak without being interrupted by five other guys.

Then they have another coffee and some cake.

Saying goodbye to Dad at the Phoenix airport was brutal. We both had tears in our eyes. I was feeling all sentimental and mushy until we were in the air seated across from the three biggest 49er fans in sports history. For two hours straight they went on about football. They talked about "Joe" like he was their best friend. They covered everything, the Cowboys, the Raiders, the overtimes, the penalties, the salaries; and then, when they ran out of facts, the skinny one started reading the sports page aloud to the two other idiots. They were getting on my nerves so bad, but, of course, they didn't bother Bill. He just sat and read his book while I suffered through this torment alone. Each paragraph of the paper brought on another national debate to be settled by the three sports geniuses. It was really hard to read Toni Morrison with sports phone blasting in your other ear. Just as I was about to say something rude like "get a life," the baby behind us started crying and drowned them all out.

Ha ha. That shut 'em up.

We came home to a box from Jackson & Perkins on our doorstep. You can't even imagine how thrilled that made me. I immediately forgave the three sports guys on the plane and went dashing into the kitchen for a knife to tear open the cardboard box. I gently pulled out my four new bare-root roses and soaked them in warm water overnight. We unpacked a little bit. Then I fell asleep with the cats and the Jackson & Perkins catalog on my pillow.

JANUARY 8

I did a little post–New Year's nature walk. The big *B* word once again, *bust*. It's green and wet and blah. A couple of bulbs are peeking up from the ground, but I can't remember which ones they are, so I can't get too excited yet. If I had labeled them correctly as perfect Martha Stewart would do, I wouldn't be in this predicament.

Cat came over to visit. She recently had a baby and is chipper and skinny. How can she possibly be skinny? I told her about the marriage proposal. I'm not sure if I'm ready for marriage. Is seven years really enough time to know? Maybe we should wait. Plus, what brilliant puritanical, Nice Nelly came up with the idea of monogamy? Like that's even remotely normal.

And what are the chances that a marriage will really last? Cat looked disappointed in me, so I shut up. She is too good to be true. She's from Indiana. In New York City we never knew people like her really existed. She's happy and nice. She gave me the phone number of a woman to talk to. Her name is Liisa and she's some kind of counselor who makes you breathe. Then she left. Right, like I have time to sit and breathe.

Instead, I sat out in the yard and brooded.

That didn't help, so I decided to call Cat's friend. I made an appointment for tomorrow. I'll tell you right now, if she's got crystals or talks about that inner child thing, I'm out of there.

It had barely stopped raining, and it was almost dark, but I had the primal urge to plant. I put on my raingear and went out into the mud. I dug four deep holes for the roses. I filled the wheelbarrow with Bill's fresh new compost and peat moss. Then I put the roses safely in their new homes, covered them up, and pleaded with them to grow.

JANUARY 10

Today I did it! I went to see 'Liisa'. (She's Finnish, not pretentious.) I drove the backroads early in the morning, through the fog. I listened to country music and related. That's always scary. The first thing I noticed when I pulled into her driveway was that her jasmine is blooming and mine isn't. Figures. I walked in very cautiously and skeptically. She's a beautiful woman and doesn't have crystals, thank God. I sat down in a big cozy chair across from her, and she asked me why I'd come. Before I could answer her, tears came rolling down my face, and I couldn't speak for about five minutes. I can't believe I was sad about this stuff again. I thought that I had worked through my imperfect childhood years ago. I mean, I talked it to death with professionals and with my girlfriends and, basically, with anyone who looked the least bit interested, until the whole topic bored me to death. Liisa just sat there watching me, and I was thinking to myself, in the middle of my tears, who the hell does she think she is not saying anything, just looking at me? Finally I spoke. I told her that my boyfriend had proposed to me and I had said yes, but that I couldn't speak the *W* word (I whispered "wedding") and that I hate the titles *husband* and *wife,* and I thought only ignorant, naive fools got married. Liisa seemed fine with all of this. She even looked as though she agreed with it, which concerned me. Then she went on about her training and how she could help me go deeper into understanding myself. Oh, great, just the person I was trying to get away from. She rambled on about the heart and the soul and the layers of the self, and about some Buddhist guy I never heard of. She asked some questions about Bill, my parents, and my sisters.

Then I went on to my favorite topic — my mother. How she ran away from her father, The Tyrant, when she was twenty years old, came to the States, learned the English language, found a job, and supported herself in a new life and country. A few years later she met my father at a party. She was wearing her glamorous green satin gown and flirting with all the guys. My father says he fell madly in love with her. She was beautiful and charming. They married. Gradually, the marriage grew complicated and sour. She says she put my father through graduate school; he says she didn't. She says he left her; he says she drove him away.

My sisters and I, at a young age, built the code of the sisterhood. When my father left, my mother took out her anger and disappointment in life on us. We had Archie comic books and Mad magazines hidden in the bathroom in case we got stuck there hiding for a few hours. Ma's temper would flare and we'd all run for cover, even Fluffy. Ma wanted my father and the family back but she sure went about it in a strange way. One minute she was angry and the next she was crying, asking the gods why he had left her. I would try to comfort her, but she wouldn't let me; it was almost as if she were in a spell. As soon as the storm was over, Ma would be in the kitchen making us a great dinner, kissing and hugging us as if nothing had ever happened.

Then Liisa made me close my eyes, breathe, and tell her what I saw. "All I see is brown, dirty, dark mud, and you're getting on my fucking nerves." She let me get up and I said goodbye. I told her I couldn't visualize or meditate, so she shouldn't her waste her time with me.

I think she may be a witch.

I got home and took a long nap. When I woke up I had the desire to paint. I haven't painted in years. I'm not very good at it, but I keep trying, thinking that one day I'll get better. I took out my acrylic paint set and painted flowers and fruit on two big clay garden pots. My grapes and oranges came out looking a little like my mother's artwork. That made me sad and I felt guilty for snitching on her to the witch.

JANUARY 13

Today I baby-sat for little Cosette. Cat had meetings all day so I got to take care of my little squishface. I'm so in love with her; I sit and stare at her for hours and can't get anything done when she's here. By 5:00 P.M. she was sick of me and wanted her mother. My feelings were hurt, but I was kind of sick of her crying too. The only thing that kept her calm the last half hour was being carried around the garden. So there I was walking in circles, around and around and around, and each time around I noticed how much more I needed to weed. I also noticed how some of the plants we pay no attention to are doing fine and that others, like some of the roses that we pamper and nurture, aren't doing a damn thing. There are about twenty bulbs coming up in the ground near the compost and in the compost bin. I never planted them. That's just so typical of our luck, to have flowers growing nowhere else but in the filthy compost bin. This is likely to upset Bill to no end.

JANUARY 20

The rainstorm has gotten so bad that the phone lines went out and I'm stuck here by myself with no one to talk to. It has been pouring rain consistently for the last three days, and today the fifty-mile-per-hour winds have kicked in. I can't help thinking this is happening because I hung up on Ma three days ago, but that's ridiculous. Isn't it? I feel really sad. I just want to be out working in the garden but it's too wet and windy to get anything done and I'd look like a nut. Wouldn't I?

Ever since I talked to Liisa, I've been more depressed than ever. I decided to put the small blue bench into a shady spot and make it "a bower dedicated to Saturn." It's what they did in Renaissance days—a place where they would go to be sad and not be bothered. You could be really alone and hide from the happy people. No one would come and try to cheer you up. They'd just leave you there in your own miserable little hell.

Last night I had nightmares about crowds and dying. I couldn't seem to get away from people. The whole circus was following me. I tried to escape on the train, but they filled up every car with all their outlandish outfits and loud, irritating voices. Then the circus turned into a film crew. Every department was complaining to me. Everyone had a big problem and felt that the whole movie depended on them alone. I mean, even the craft service person! Where do they get such audacity? Such egos. Then Ma, the Queen Bee arrived. She was waving a fan and saying, "Open a window, I can't breathe, eeouph . . . It smells in here, get all these people out of here, they stink. Who are they anyway? They don't look normal."

In my next dream, after I got off of the circus train, I was running down the street in the middle of the night. I had on my Barbie pajamas, and I was in Palo Alto. Gwyneth was in her old celadon Volkswagon van on the corner of University and it was five in the morning. She was listening to Michael Nyman and smoking a French cigarette. She waved. I jumped into the van and we cuddled up in the front seat and had a deep conversation about the torment of love. Her Volkswagon was the only vehicle on this empty, misty street. The annoying opera music was screeching out of the van windows along with her smoke rings. A street sweeper truck came along and swept the street and waved to us in slow motion. I loved this moment. I loved Gwyneth, but the music was driving me crazy and her cigarette was making me sick, so I jumped out of the van. Then I woke up.

I went into the kitchen to make some warm milk. It was only 1:00 A.M. It felt much later. I decided to call my friend Barbara, in Colorado, because she's always up late and that in itself impresses me. Her dad was recently diagnosed with liver cancer. Just like that. One day he was fine, the next he was in chemotherapy. She had just spent a week with him. Her parents have been divorced for a long time. Her dad is remarried, and his second wife doesn't like the fact that he's still friendly with his first wife. When are these people going to get over themselves? How can people in their sixties still be so selfish? Didn't they find the wisdom that age brings?

Don't they get it?

Barbara changed the subject and started torturing me for information about the big day. I told her that I didn't think I was going to make it to my *W* (wedding) day because I was having too many nightmares. She told me once again what a good catch I was and how she hopes that one day she can meet a man like me. We said goodnight, and she said that she loves me. It always means a lot to me when Barbara says "I love you" because I know she doesn't toss those words around loosely the way I do but only says them to very special people in her life. It's now 2:00 A.M. The lightning keeps causing the kitchen lights to flicker on and off, and up in the skylight is the pitter-patter of the rain, with the moon shining through. I sit here drinking my warm milk and honey, hoping that Barbara will be able to spend quality time with her father, in peace, before he dies.

JANUARY 23

It's been raining for a week now. I haven't written much. I haven't been out in the garden. It's too wet and windy even for me to be puttering around aimlessly. I'm home making soup and watching the wind toss over the trellis with the honeysuckle on it.

Yesterday was Elissa's birthday. We splurged and got her a facial. Then we went to a matinee. We saw *Immortal Beloved,* a story about Ludwig van Beethoven. We were both so moved by it; it was a pure masterpiece. There is a scene in it that stayed with me. It is where Ludwig is standing on stage with the symphony orchestra playing his emotionally charged "Ode to Joy." The scene cuts back and forth between his old age and his youth in a dreamy flashback of a young boy running away from his abusive father. He has escaped through a window and is running and running and running on a cool clear night until he reaches a lake. He throws off his nightshirt and floats in the water under a brilliant sky filled with stars. He has finally triumphed and found peace.

JANUARY 24

All this rain is depressing us. The other day I told Bill he was a pessimist and that he sees the glass half empty, so now he's really milking it. Every morning he wakes me up by going, "Ppssss. . . ." I grumble, "What?" He says, "Babe, guess what? It's raining."

JANUARY 25

It was basically a torrential downpour today, but not even the storm from hell could keep me away from meeting the Rose Man! Tonight I drove through the loudest raindrops ever, to Book Passage to hear Rayford Reddell speak about his eight thousand rosebushes. Yes, eight thousand! Believe it, baby. A few years ago, Bill and I were out cycling along Pepper Road in Petaluma, and found his ranch by accident. It is a spectacular sight, and there really are thousands of roses. This was before my neurosis with gardening, and I remember thinking, he sure is obsessed with roses — not normal.

Anyway, fifty other gardening dweebs were also there to hear him speak. I felt as though I was at some kind of AA meeting and that we would each have to stand up. We'd have to testify that we drove through the biggest storm to hit California in ten years because we were sick and obsessed with roses and needed help. I was worse than most because I got there an hour early so I could get a front-row seat (goody-goody). I was wearing my black leather jacket, chewing gum, and sitting with my feet up on a side bench trying to look cool so that I wouldn't appear to be a biddy, when two nuns came and sat next to me. I got all quiet and softly smiled as if we were in a church or the library. I straightened myself up, tossed out the gum, and took out my notepad. If only Bill could have seen me! The closest I've ever, ever been to a real nun! I was giggling away inside, but then I thought that maybe there was a message here, that I should take it a little more seriously, and I started worrying about the drive home.

Ray was an inspiration. We all watched him with admiration like he was some kind of god. He explained the entire process they use to grow roses at Garden Valley Ranch and said if we did all of these things, our roses were sure to succeed. He also admitted speaking to his roses and that made me happy. He suggested that we strip all the leaves from the rosebushes after the storm. A week or two later we should prune correctly as he showed in his video: Cut with shears face down and on a slant; prune off at least half of most rosebushes; close to two-thirds of the plant is even better (the nuns gasped!). This is very daring, but he told us to be brave, and I trust Ray. Then take dormant spray and spray all your rosebushes so they have some help against diseases such as powdery mildew, black spot, and rust. In March, begin fertilizing and cross your fingers, and that's it. Piece of cake!

Next was the question and answer period. Those nuns kept raising their hands so much that he never even picked on me! He must have sinned in his life and feels that by answering all their stupid questions he'll be saved. This was really pissing me off. The nuns asked some okay questions about which roses to plant and I copied all of their information because they wrote faster than I did. (I cheated! I copied off of nuns. Yahoo!) Climbing Iceberg was the easiest and most prolific climber suggested. Then came Cecile Brunner, Golden Showers, Madame Alfred Carriere, and Zephirine Drouhin'. (Oh, if only my sisters could hear these names . . .) Other rosebushes that Ray highly recommended were: Heritage, Bibi Maizoon, Bianca, Bewitched, Europeana, and Bonica.

Then Ray signed his new book, and these pushy, nebby-nose gardeners kept lining up there and asking even more questions about their stupid gardens, and I never had a chance to ask my own menial, self-centered questions. What a bust!

I drove home listening to the loud pitter-patter of the rain and the ferocious wind. I thought about the nuns and wondered what their garden looks like. Is it spectacular? Does everything bloom all year long?

Do they get special treatment from God?

Figures.

JANUARY 26

Last night, before we went to bed, Bill and I began making a few minor decisions about the wedding. It was a short conversation, and we both rushed through it nonchalantly as though we were discussing the weather. Then we went to sleep. This morning we both woke up from nightmares. I didn't remember mine until Bill told me that he had dreamed that he had a severely infectious disease and had been sent to Staten Island to be quarantined for months. Then I remembered having dreamed that I was having a heart-to-heart chat with Adam Chandler on his show and I was telling him that I had only one day left to live and was going to spend it at my favorite nursery.

After we agreed that our dreams were filled with escape and avoidance, we had a grapefruit and my usual burnt toast, and planned our weekend.

JANUARY 27

I sent Bill to the supermarket and asked him to pick up an interesting and exciting vegetable we don't often eat. He came home with celery.

This concerns me.

JANUARY 28

We had a few hours of clear weather so I finally got outside to prune the rosebushes. I love, love, love, pruning things. I think that people who enjoy pruning are really self-destructive and need help. I decided to be brave and prune all the rosebushes severely. I mixed some compost, leaves, and redwood bark to make a good mulch and made a hill of mulch at the bottom of each rosebush. Then I talked to them and gave them some encouragement. Maui thought I was talking to her and came over. I told her that we renamed her last night, but only temporarily. Bill and I were watching Sonny Bono pretending to know what he was doing in the political arena on TV, and we both wanted to hurl. Bill was very depressed. He said the only thing that would make him happy was to change Maui's name to Sonny. So we did. Bill is smiling again.

JANUARY 29

I planted some more bare-root roses. I had to sneak them in before Bill caught me in the act. He was inside glued to the 49ers game, so I was safe for a couple of hours. He doesn't have my passion for roses and thinks they're too much work. Once they get all their little diseases in the summer, I sort of agree with him and I'm ready to throw them all away, but then they recover and look beautiful again, and I fall back in love. I planted two English roses: the Pilgrim (yellow) and Gertrude Jekyll (pink). This is the first time I've planted the old-fashioned English type of rose. They've always been my favorite, but I thought they were too hard to care for. This will be the test. It started raining again while I was outside planting, but that didn't stop me. I was already soaked and full of mud. I didn't want any of the neighbors to catch me out there and think I was deranged. Just then, little Rebecca, next door, opened her front door, stomped her foot, and yelled out to me, "Annie, what—are–you–doing?" I stood there in the pouring rain trying to look sane and said, "Oh, just things, I'm just doing things." Rebecca slammed the door closed. I'm sure she went in to tattletale on me to her mother.

JANUARY 30

I sprayed the roses with dormant spray today. Bill, Ron, and Mr. Louie were screaming inside the house as the 49ers won yet another Superbowl. The men interviewed had tears in their eyes. For years I've tried to give Bill something to cry about! Nothing has worked. I just don't understand what is so emotional about kicking around a ball, but I do think it is good simply to have men cry.

I think it's a good sign for humanity.

February

FEBRUARY 1

My mother and I share a love of politics. We believe that our friends Bill and Hillary are doing a fine job, especially while being surrounded by wolves, snakes, and cockroaches. Today I received two articles in the mail from Ma. The first was about the Republican dream to get rid of "big government," which really means they want to replace it with "big business." On the top of the article Ma wrote, "Mouse, something's wrong with these people. Your mother." Now, I agree our government isn't always perfect, but I do believe that big business certainly needs to be under careful scrutiny. Their first concern, after all, is not about the consumer's well-being but about how much money they can make off the consumer. Without the Food and Drug Administration or the Environmental Protection Agency, America would be a walking disaster of disease and pollution. Do they really believe we can trust big industry to do the right thing? Like they care about the air or the land or the water? *Really care?*

The second article from Ma was about Newt Gingrich, family values, and tax reform. On this one she wrote, "Mouse, here's your friend. Love, Mommy." It started out about Newt's family values. How he left his wife and two kids. How they took him to court for child support and the church had to take up a collection for his family. Then the article went on to tax reform and how anyone making more than $200,000 annually would save money and the rest of us working-class losers would pay higher taxes. You know it's exactly like Ma always said: "The rich get richer and the poor get poorer." I would love to set my mother loose on the right-wing religious militia. Let her enter the room giving her loud and passionate "It's a man's world" speech. She'd kick some serious butt, and by the time she got to the best part, the "How dare you?" part, she'd have the freshmen congresspeople running for their lives.

FEBRUARY 2

It rained most of the weekend, again. I took lots of naps in between reading *Bastard out of Carolina,* then I listened to the hard raindrops fall on the kitchen skylight, waiting for it to break and splatter all over and flood the house. But it never happened, thank God. Bill lay next to me, shaking his head. He was reading a magazine article about first-year gardens. Some of the pictures were extraordinary. We decided that they could not possibly be first-year gardens. These people are either on drugs or big, fat liars!

Well, that about sums up the weekend.

Today the sun peeked out in between the showers. Every time I came inside it got sunny and the second I went back out into the garden it started drizzling. Max followed me in and out of the house, back and forth. Maui just watched us from the bedroom window, pretending she wasn't interested, but I kept catching her peeking at us with one eye.

I managed to prune the fuchsias back to their main branches. It's supposed to help new growth come in. Yeah, right. We'll see. Then I planted twenty-five gladiolas along the side fence in front of the cherry tree. Gladiolas, Ma's favorite flower—after roses, of course.

After that I came inside to have some "almost as good as Ma's" chicken soup that I'd made over the weekend. It'll never be as great as hers, but I'm getting a little closer each try. Today I miss her and remember how she took care of us when we were sick. She would squish us into the bed, tuck us tightly under the blankets, then rub our backs, smooth our hair, and kiss us on the cheek. Then she'd go make us the best drippy soft-boiled eggs and chicken soup. These were times when her true love for us shined through, even though she was still mad at Daddy and the world. Once, when we were eight, Ca was really sick and we decided we'd have so much more fun if I got sick too and got to stay home with her and play. So Ca made me stand on my head after dinner for twenty minutes to get me to throw up, and my mother came in the room and caught us. Once again, I got blamed for Ca's brilliant ideas.

I sat down to eat my chicken soup and watched the rain. I found the wishbone. When we were in high school, I was usually the last one to stay at the dinner table, because everyone else had left in a huff. My mother would pull out the wishbone from under her napkin, close her eyes, and wish. We would have a few special moments of silence. For years I took this ritual very seriously and would close my eyes tight and concentrate very hard on magical, unrealistic, naive notions. I wished that life wouldn't make me angry, that the world's bitterness wouldn't seep into my skin, and that someday someone would come to save me.

My wish came true the day I met Bill.

I met him seven years ago, at Ca's graduation from chiropractic school. A few weeks later he wrote to me saying he'd be in New York on his way to Europe. We spent a week together. It was wonderful, but I was still in my self-destructive stage, and he was too normal. Still, it could possibly have worked out, so naturally I ran like hell. Six months later I finally escaped New York City and moved to California to be with Ca. I didn't think I was serious about Bill, but when I saw him again that day in Golden Gate Park, I realized that he just might be what I needed. He invited me to his cabin for the weekend and I dumped Ca in about five seconds. He called it his mountain chalet, but I'd say it was more like a couple of pieces of wood put together around old, creaky furniture and a wood stove. The cabin was surrounded by the most trees I'd ever seen in my life. There were pine trees and a sky full of stars. I hated it! It scared me to death. I had just left New York City and I couldn't handle it. On top of the isolation, we had to carry bags of food and our luggage uphill through three feet of snow, about a quarter mile to even get to the crusty cabin. So there I am bitching to myself as I'm trudging through what seems like an avalanche to a New Yorker, in the middle of the night, freezing and sweating at the same time. And there's Bill singing to himself and going on about smelling the fresh mountain air. I'm thinking to myself that this relationship will not work, no *way*, and what excuse can I use to get the hell out tomorrow morning. I was also trying to look good; to look like I knew what I was doing. But every time he turned around to check on me, I was stuck in snowbanks trying to gracefully lift myself and my city-girl luggage and look sexy at the same time.

Mr. Louie and Pucci were with us and took everything in stride, so I had to keep my shock and anger to myself. The next morning, we learned that the water pipes had frozen and there was no hot water. There was also no firewood, so Pucci and I were sent out to collect firewood, while the men fixed the water pipes. Pucci, once again, took this development in stride, so I didn't complain. She kept going on about how much she loved Mr. Louie and how lucky we were to be in the wilderness. Is she out of her fucking mind? All I wanted to do at that moment was dump Bill and get back to CIVILIZATION! When we got back to the cabin, Bill asked me to make a fire, and I said sure, but in New York I had never ever touched real firewood. I had no idea what the hell I was doing. I think he realized this and came over to help. It was the first time I had experienced the "rocket scientist" side of him. He explained each step slowly and meticulously, and, instead of getting on my nerves, I fell deeply in love with him.

After breakfast, Bill took us out cross-country skiing for six hours, uphill to Sardine Lake in a goddamn blizzard! Now I hated his guts again and was devising my escape with every push and glide I took. At the fifth hour, my skis got slower and my legs were throbbing. My true self, which I had been hiding from him, came bursting out (I call it the "Sha" side of my personality). I had a temper tantrum right there in the middle of the fucking forest, in front of his two best friends in the whole wide world. I'm sure they were wondering what Bill saw in me and why he had such poor judgment in women. I screamed about how I HATED EVERYTHING about the wilderness and was dying to go back to New York City, where people did normal things! I wasn't moving another inch because I wasn't a triathlete like him and I was simply exhausted like any sane person would be.

I think this might've been the pivotal point in my friendship with Mr. Louie. All respect between us died as I yelled and he yelled back and made fun of me. He had the audacity to imitate me and then he called me the New York Bitch From Hell. That just did it. From that day on there's been a war between us. In between all the harassment, Bill quietly took my skis, put wax on them, and handed them back to me. He said: "Babe, whatever you want to do is fine," and I melted. He slowed down and I followed him silently for the last mile, whimpering to myself.

When we got back to the Neanderthal cabin, the keeper of the lodge gave us more assignments to do. They call this a vacation? After digging the cars out of the snow, we were finally allowed hot showers, but only for three minutes each. I hogged all of Bill's water allotment and then we went upstairs to make passionate love. This was the best part of the whole trip; everything else basically sucked. The next morning at sunrise, after staying up almost all night talking and kissing in the moonlight, I told him I loved him. He said it back without freaking out. This was new for me, because all the boys before him thought if they uttered the words *I love you*, their little bitty heads might fall off or something.

By 8:00 A.M. Bill had me out shoveling snow again with Pucci. There we were digging our cars out of the snow that had fallen during the night. Mr. Louie had the only shovel because he hogged it right away, of course, so the rest of us had to use kitchen utensils. This was not fun, and I was miserable and thinking again about dumping Bill. First of all, you had to ski or snowshoe the quarter mile to the car with your weapon of attack in your hand, then dig snow, then hike uphill through three feet of snow back to the house to get all of your luggage and the garbage and carry it down the slope on your skis, again. (I couldn't wait to get to a phone and tattletale to Ca what Bill had put me through. In fact, the only thing that made me smile was thinking what Sha would've done in this situation. I think some lives would have been in serious danger.) Pucci wasn't feeling well. As she was shoveling she started feeling like she was coming down with the flu. She was pissed! Yay! I was so happy that I finally had someone on my side, and we became best friends instantly. She swore she would never come back to Bill's cabin again!! I instigated a big fight between her and John. She was so mad at him, she wouldn't let him listen to the football game during the four-hour car ride home!

I smell victory!

FEBRUARY 5

The rain has ended — for now. Some of the daffodils have blossomed early. They look very happy, and I'm so proud of them for making it through all the storms. I thanked them each individually and then started weeding the rose garden. It was a mess from the storms. I spent an hour out there and only accomplished a quarter of the work to be done. I was thinking about Ga. The garden she had with Bob was my inspiration for a garden. Years ago, when I was visiting Texas, Bob showed me how to turn the soil and prepare it for planting. All I remember thinking was, what a bunch of work this is and why doesn't this guy get a life. I mean, right, like I'm gonna get out my pitchfork and shovel and dig a hole. Then, a few months later, Ga sent me pictures of her perfect eggplants, colorful lettuces, dahlias, really red tomatoes, peppers, giant roses, and amazing watermelons. I was so impressed. It was just like magic and I wanted it.

When Bob passed away, my mother left New York and went to live with Ga. We thought it would be nice for them to have each other's company. It was good for a short time, but soon enough they began to drive each other absolutely crazy. Ga put in a rose garden for Ma. My mom was in pain from her health problems, but she still got excited about the roses blooming. She would call me and report that another rose was blooming. Every week during the summer, she would name a rose after each of her four daughters. Whoever was on her good side that week got the biggest and best rose named after her. This may not have meant much to my sisters because they were too busy, but since I was the goody-goody, when it came my turn to be chosen for rose-of-the-week, I was honored. I knew that loving each rose was her way of showing she loved us, even if she was yelling at us at the same time.

Ga was a saint; she took the best care of Ma. She tried over and over to make her happy. Ma wanted Ga to be a party girl and attend social events and have lots of dates. I guess all mothers want that. But Ga is an intellectual. She has a Ph.D. and she loves teaching and she's out there educating, and that's what the world needs more of anyway. She's head of organizations for the advancement of women, multiculturalism, and world peace. This gets on Ma's nerves. She wants her to find a guy. Without going into the gruesome details, their very different outlooks on life soon made for an unhealthy living situation.

Recently Ga was offered a teaching position away from Dallas, which she accepted, so Ma will go live in San Diego, near Ca. She'll move out by the end of the month. We're all so excited about this fresh start for both Ga and Ma, but most of all Sha and I are happy that Ca got a big karmic-kickback.

You see, for years Ca got away with murder. She didn't have to wash the dishes, vacuum, set the table, take out garbage, do laundry, or do food shopping. She was the brilliant twin. I was the goody-two-shoes. Ca was either too busy studying or practicing the piano to do *any* chores. Now that we've grown up, sort of, Ma still lets Ca get away with stuff. I don't know why. Maybe Ma respects her because she's a doctor, or maybe she's afraid of her because sometimes Ca can be bitchy.

FEBRUARY 8

After raking billions and billions of leaves into the compost, Bill said we still needed more. Sometimes he gets on my very last nerve. He sent me over to the neighbor's house to confiscate the leaves from their driveway. After leaf duty, he cleaned out the shed and dragged out his tree spraying warfare and attacked the diseased peach tree. It has had peach blight and peach leaf curl for the last two years. We spray it with copper a couple of times each year but it still puts out tasteless, deformed peaches. While Bill sprayed, I pruned the lemon, apple, and fig trees. I had just seen astonishing statistics on CNN that fifty-five thousand women are raped each month in America. This filled me with so much anger that I may have gone a bit overboard in pruning the poor, innocent fruit trees.

FEBRUARY 10

I saw Liisa again today. I had PMS, I was tired, and I wanted to kill her. I had absolutely nothing to say, so she made me breathe. I didn't want to breathe and got cranky. She probably hates me and thinks I'm just another miserable New Yorker who wants to walk around angry at the world and doesn't really ever want to be happy anyway. But in the middle of all this silly breathing, I decided that I do want to be happy; I'm tired of hating everyone and everything. Liisa asked me what I was thinking, and I said, "I decided that I shouldn't wear so much black." She told me about a sale on colorful turtlenecks at the mall. I can't believe Ms. Zen Woman talked fashion with me! I'm so excited that even she has shallow potential and knows a good sale when she sees one! I just love that!

On the drive home, through Nicasio Valley, singing along with Marvin Gaye, I saw three enormous, miraculous rainbows stretching over the hills. I stopped the car in front of the old Nicasio Church and watched the rainbows till they faded away. When

I got home there was a message from Sha with a new diet ice cream tip and, on top of that, the first camellia ever to show its face blossomed in our garden! It's beautiful pink on the outside and yellow on the inside. I can't believe it ever did anything. It's been sitting there like a useless old bump on a log for two years, accompanied by the bust rhododendrons.

FEBRUARY 11

Today Sha is back in New York for an anniversary party at the the Bottom Line, a jazz club. She was a coatcheck girl there when she was seventeen. The Bottom Line meant a lot to all of us in our youth because we used to go there to hide from the world. Every time that there was another civil war in our house, I would usually let Ma cry on my shoulder for an hour or so, then Ca and I would take the express train to the Village. We'd work with Sha in the coatcheck room and see all the shows for free. Sometimes they even fed us! At midnight we'd all ride the train home together afraid to walk in the door. Ma was in tremendous emotional pain back then, and we never knew what mood she would be in.

Sometimes the New York City subway seemed safer than the hallways of our home.

FEBRUARY 14

Today is Valentine's Day. I got a card for Bill that says, "Back home we have a name for men who don't do something romantic for their womanfolk on Valentine's Day. Dead Meat." Before Bill was in my life, Valentine's Day meant a call from my mother to tell me how beautiful I was and how much she loved me. At night I would sit and eat a pint of chocolate ice cream listening to Patsy Cline singing "She's Got You."

But today it meant waking up in the morning, next to Bill,

hearing Van Morrison singing "Someone Like You." For dinner we had heart-shaped pasta and I looked into Bill's eyes for a long time because that always gets on his nerves.

Bill had mail-ordered a gardenia plant for me. The picture on the box was splendid, and it's supposed to arrive already blooming, so we got all excited because we've had no luck with gardenias. Not like that should surprise us. We opened it up, and it was just another bust green ol' thang with zero blooms that looks like the plastic plants at Target for $2.99. We called the company up and they said to just keep the plant free of charge, so we did. We'll give it a few months, then it's outta here.

FEBRUARY 16

This weekend Bill helped me weed the rose garden. It went so much faster with two people working at it. (Anyone that will come help you weed your garden is a true friend and should not be taken for granted.) I'm so used to being out here by myself talking to the roses. You have to talk to your roses. I keep telling Bill how great the roses are going to look this summer. I sure hope I'm right. At one point I looked up to stretch my neck and there was Maui sunbathing on the peach tree. She was watching us slave away in the garden. Then she yawned.

Sunday we went for the first bike ride of the New Year. We rode near Nicasio for about two hours. There is something very mystical about the land out there. It is so beautiful, and you feel blessed to be breathing in fresh coastal air. We stopped in Point Reyes, read the paper, looked in the nursery downtown, and rode home yelling at the cows to get a life. Talk about lazy animals. We shared a Power Bar near the ranch that has all the goats, sheep, and little rabbits. The mustard fields around us were so spectacular that we felt like we were in the *Wizard of Oz*. I really believe that cycling is the answer to a bad mood—it is such a high. You get out there, get a good pace going, and you feel that you could conquer the world. When I first started dating Bill, I had

a three-speed bike from the flea market. Here was Mr. Triathlete taking me cycling in the Santa Cruz hills. Each time we went
out riding together I would curse him out the whole way up the
hills. He did it on purpose. He would get just far enough away
from me that he couldn't hear me and happily pedal away. And
I'd be there hating his guts, yelling and threatening him and then
begging him to go get the car, drive me home, and let me out of
his life. A year later we were still together, but we saved up and
bought me a good ten-speed road bike, and ever since then, I've
been hooked.

FEBRUARY 17

What is up with all these award shows? I swear, every two
weeks there's some kind of new made-up award and a big tele-
vised Hollywood extravaganza. I don't see any other profession
getting it's big, fat ego fed so consistently. Don't these people have
anything better to do than pat themselves on the back every
other week? Could they get a life? Is that too much to ask?

FEBRUARY 18

The Queen Bee is out of Texas! The state will never be the
same again. She's staying at Ca's for a few days until her apartment is ready. She sounds happy. The weird thing is we can't find
Ga. She called Ca and told her that she was going away to get
some rest for a few days. Ca doesn't remember what she said to
her because it was seven in the morning and Ca is bitchy at that
time of day. She also wrote down the wrong number because she
was half asleep. Now, of course, Ma blames this all on Ga.

Do you see how Ca gets away with everything!?

No one has heard from Ga all week, and in this nebby-nose
family that's highly unusual. Her colleague at the university said
that she went to Colorado to see the pope! Now we think she's

joined a religious cult! Hey, this is getting kind of juicy. If she doesn't call Ma on Saturday, she'll be in major trouble. Ma doesn't care if we're big shots or how busy we might be, we have to fit it into our schedules to call her on Saturday morning or she simply assumes that we're dead.

FEBRUARY 20

I saw Liisa, the witch, this morning. She talked about layers and darkness. It wasn't fun seeing her. I was in a negative mood. I said, "If marriage is so great, why is everyone going around having affairs and 50 percent of marriages end in divorce?" To punish me for my negativity, she made me do more breathing. Of course, when I left her house, I felt hopeful, like I always seem to feel after I see her. I also felt kind of foggy and out of it. I guess I was, because I missed the turnoff and ended up in Point Reyes. I went to my secret beach and watched the sunset. I thought about all the times my parents had taken us to Jones Beach when we were little. We have so many pictures of us in our little sun hats and bathing suits, laughing, building sand castles and chocolate sand pies. I wonder if my parents were happy back then? Does the unhappiness in a marriage creep up slowly or does it just burst forth one day out of nowhere?

FEBRUARY 21

Praise the lord. Ga has been found and she hasn't been kidnapped by a religious cult. She went to rest at her friend's house in Illinois, and because Ca had written down the wrong phone number, we couldn't get in touch with her. Ma, naturally, refused to blame Ca. She never blames her. She excused Ca, as she always does, by telling us she "works like a dog." Ga is going to sell the house in Texas and start a new life teaching philosophy at a university in Illinois. It's really exciting. She sounds like she's twenty years old again. No more people to take care of. Finally she can be free and spoil herself, because "she works like a dog too." I sent her a good luck card today. It had "Sartre's Shopping List" on it, consisting of things like cigarettes, Pepto-Bismol, a new beret, etc., etc. Then at the bottom, it said "Oh, what's the use. . . ."

That's kind of how I feel.

FEBRUARY 22

I was talking on the phone to Sha and stopped in the middle of my story because I noticed that something is . . . BLOOMING!!! The Hardenbergia vine out on the deck is bursting with purple flowers. It's absolutely stunning. I told Sha I'd call her back later after I examined this new botanical development a bit more closely. I stood out there staring at it in disbelief when I noticed ol' granny, at the upstairs window next door, watching me. I pretended to be doing something constructive, like watering the herbs even though it's been pouring rain for three weeks straight.

I called Sha back to finish telling her about *Hotel Pastis*, the book I was reading. It's about an executive who retires from the advertising business and renovates an old inn in the South of France. It's full of gorgeous descriptions of roads and towns around Provence intertwined with ridiculous stories about the cutthroat advertising business. The characters are hysterical, and they reminded me of when Sha worked at one of those big fancy ad agencies on Madison Avenue many years ago. She would come home from work wiped out and fed up with the whole world. (She *also* worked like a dog.) On these occasions I stayed far away from her because I knew right away that she'd had another "Mickey's thumb" day. This meant that lots of high paid, highly educated, grown-up men and a few women sat in a smoky conference room for many painstaking hours of laborious arguing to decide where to put Mickey's thumb on a print ad for some soft drink! Hel*lo?* Like who cares?

Sha sat through these meetings in total disbelief that she was still on the planet Earth. Don't you see? This is what's wrong with the world. Don't they get it? It starts right here and goes on and on and on. The whole problem in a nutshell—it's all about Mickey's thumb!

FEBRUARY 23

It was still light out, and I had been reading about dahlias in *Horticulture* magazine, so I went out to the nursery to check this flower out. The article says how easy they are to care for and how they can grow up to six feet. It says they bloom in ninety days. Like, I believe that. I bought four of them anyway; two decorative and two cactus. They look absolutely gorgeous on the package, and I always fall for that and pray to the gods that make the flowers bloom that mine will look maybe even just half as good. I could be happy with that.

I planted them according to the picky-poky directions. You have to plant the tuber horizontally with the eye pointing toward the stake and cover it with three inches of soil. As shoots grow, you fill the rest of the hole. (Like I have time for this. . . .) Just as I finished, the sun started setting and ominous clouds were coming in above. The sky quickly became charcoal gray, and the wind began swinging the garden gate back and forth. This frightened the wimpy cats, and they had to get out of their cozy, little, napping spots and run around like they had somewhere to go, or all of a sudden had a purpose for living.

Fat chance.

FEBRUARY 24

Today Bill's mother came to visit. She's a sixty-something-year-old great-grandmother who travels around visiting people with her Rollerblades and her diabetic cat, Bebe. I took her to my aerobics class. She's twice my age. I guess the fifty squats and twenty-five pushups didn't bother her, because she just kept on smiling and pumping away, like she was having a ball. She made me sick, actually. I won't work out with her again.

When we got home, she gave her spoiled little rugrat cat an insulin shot along with moist, yummy, canned cat food. This bothered Bill and me tremendously. Maui and Max were watching all this affection, and I'm afraid they may start wondering why they get generic, dry cat food and why we don't speak to them in high-pitched, cutesy tones. All this was too much for me so I went out to look at the garden and left Bill alone with Ma talking about religion. When I came back inside the garage, spoiled little Bebe was eating Maui and Max's boring, dry cat food and they were "happy as clams," eating her fancy, moist canned food. This made my day.

FEBRUARY 25

A.M.   The headlines today said ten billion people too many. The average birthrate in the United States is 2.1 children per family. In Saudi Arabia, it is 6.4, and in India, it is 8.5. The prediction for the year 2100 is a worldwide scene of "absolute misery, poverty, disease, and starvation."

Oh, what's the use. . . .

P.M.   Well, I mowed the lawn for the first time this year and it was quite a fiasco. Due to the winter storms, the grass was close to two feet high. I had mowed the backyard and about half the front yard, when the lawn mower fizzled out and died. I put gas in it, and that didn't help, so I went in the shed to find the lawn mower manual. This took awhile, and I could just hear Bill saying, "Put it in an easy place to find so it's there when you need it." I finally found it under cans of paint and bags of fertilizer. At this point, I wasn't in the mood to read directions. I just wanted to get the other half of the lawn done.

But I made myself sit down and read the lawn mower maintenance manual. This was torture, so I just looked at the pictures. Somehow I deciphered that it needed oil. I found some oil in the garage. At this point, I was so proud of myself. What a modern woman! I was beaming. I put the oil in and pulled the motor cord, feeling all self-satisfied. It started, but it made a loud growl and began smoking like it was about to blow up! I polluted the entire block in about thirty seconds. I turned it off and was surrounded by a cloud of dark, chemical dust. I didn't care so much about me, but I ran to the rose garden and began waving a shmata in the air so the roses wouldn't breathe in any carcinogens. Through the clouds I could see our cute neighbor, Rich, walking over. I just wanted to die.

He was smiling. He said, "Looks like you could use some help!"

I said, "Oh, no . . . I know what I'm doing, really. I'm fine. Sort of. Okay, well, maybe I'm not. I don't know what I did to this piece of shit. I'm going to get a new one in the morning." He asked me a few questions about what I had done and told me with a straight, polite face that I had put the oil in the carburetor instead of the oil fill tank. I stood there astonished and embarrassed.

Now we're going to have to move.

Before I could think of something brilliant to say, Rich started up the mower and aired out the carburetor for a few minutes so I could finish the lawn. He had it aimed right at the rose garden! I chased him around in the middle of black smoke clouds and deafening motor noise waving my arms frantically and yelling at him to get away from my roses! Then I thanked him and made him swear to god that he would never tell anyone that this incident had occurred. I watched him walk across the street and could see his shoulders quivering just a little too much. He was definitely laughing.

FEBRUARY 26

I've been on the computer for two days straight, working on a shooting schedule for a CD-ROM. I couldn't wait to get outside in the garden and away from a computer screen. I ran out the back door and did a couple of spins, because I just found out Gwyneth is available to do this project with me! That means lots of spins and sophisticated digressions from work.

Good news! Loads of narcissus are blooming their little happy faces around the yard. The jessamine vine is beginning to take off on the deck. The fragrant, yellow flowers are just starting. And this is just the beginning! On top of that, Daddy is coming out in two weeks, to plan the *W*. He sounded so cheerful. It made me a little excited. For a moment I think I was even a happy bride. But that passed and I became comfortable in my little rut once again.

I raked up a ton of grass, left over from my lawn-mowing extravaganza, and put it into the compost. Bill says I don't take composting seriously. I guess I don't. But today I'm going to start. Compost is the key to healthy soil and healthy soil is the key to the whole garden. If you don't have good soil, you may as well hang it all up and stop wasting your time. Believe me, I've learned this the hard way.

Next I spent an hour cutting apart the old honeysuckle and tossing it into the compost. The trellis had fallen down during the storm last month. The honeysuckle had been ripped from its roots for weeks but it was still alive! It just didn't want to die. I know some people like that. The good ones die and the pain-in-the-ass ones stick around forever. Figures.

I fed the azaleas and the rhododendrons with iron. On top of being bust and not blooming, they're turning yellow. I'm not sure what to do next. I never talk to them, and that may be part of the problem. I'm too busy spoiling the roses, and I guess they feel neglected. Tom Jones was singing on the transistor radio on the deck. Somehow I must've turned to my mother's station. It made me laugh out loud. When I was eight years old, in my prime goody-goody stage, I used to sing "It's Not Unusual" with my mother. We would sing and dance and laugh together. While Sha and Ga were dancing to the Rolling Stones, and Ca was buying Beatles albums, I was in the kitchen listening to Tom Jones and Julie Andrews with Ma, setting the table or doing something equally pathetic.

FEBRUARY 27

Today I planted twenty-five gladiolas and ten calla lilies along the fence. If you plant gladiolas every fifteen days you get a succession of blooms. Well, that's what it says on the package. They're always so enthusiastic on the package. Must be written by simple, little, chipper people in the Midwest.

More narcissus are blooming next to the flowering magnolia tree. This gives me hope and lets me know that spring is just around the corner. When I came inside from a productive afternoon in the garden, there was a message from Barbara. Her father died yesterday from cancer. Her stepmother, the second wife, was still making a scene at the deathbed; mad because the first wife cared. You'd think that grown-ups would get over the bullshit by that age and let people live and die in peace. She obviously has issues. You gotta work out those issues or they'll haunt you and make you a miserable person. If I'm still bitching about my childhood at sixty, somebody please put me out of my misery and just end it!

I had dreams about death last night. I was holding Barbara and she was crying. Then I dreamed that I hadn't been productive enough in my life and was off schedule. (This is a real nightmare for everyone in our family.) Just as I was about to wake up, I had an old flashback of skinny-dipping with my mother. Sha had been housesitting for some fancy music producer in upstate New York. She wasn't allowed guests, but she sneaked Ma and me in because the house was too big and scary for her alone. It was sunset on a hot August night. Sha was up on the deck, grilling chicken. Ma and I were swimming laps in the olympic-size swimming pool and laughing about living in luxury for a weekend. Then my mother took off her bathing suit and let it float away in the pool. So I did the same, and it felt great! We laughed and splashed around some more and waved to Sha. She couldn't tell that we were naked from so far above the pool. This cracked us up even more because if she had known we were skinny-dipping, she would have certainly thrown us out.

FEBRUARY 28

Bill and I had another wild Saturday night. It was about ten o'clock and we decided to look at our garden after dark so the neighbors wouldn't see us. We bundled up in layers and went outside with flashlights. Each time we saw headlights coming toward us, we turned off the flashlights and ducked until the coast was clear. To our amazement and disgust, almost everything was covered with snails and slugs! We got out the diatomaceous earth and powdered the snail paths to the plants. Diatomaceous earth is less toxic than most snail baits, so this is our first choice for attack. Then we had the snail toss contest! We wanted to see who could throw them the farthest and make the loudest noise! Maui and Max were the judges. They chased them down the street, sniffed them, and ran back to us for the next toss. Tonight Bill won, thirty to seventeen.

March

MARCH 1

Today is the first of March and spring is in the air! I can feel the nurseries, bursting with color, definitely calling my name. I drove by Sloat, the local nursery, and all sorts of flowers were blooming. I was late for an appointment so I couldn't stop in and wander around aimlessly the way I like to do. When I got home, I fed the roses with a high-nitrogen fertilizer; nitrogen is the most important element during the growing season because it stimulates growth. The roses all have lots of beautiful new, healthy leaves and some buds on them. It's giving me hope that they may actually bloom. I also fed the fuchsias and the lemon tree with a nitrogen fertilizer. Soon I will have to feed an acid fertilizer to the azaleas and rhododendrons; after they bloom (*if* they bloom). You lose your patience waiting for some plants to do anything, while others try to please you every second. For example, we hardly pay any attention to coreopsis, a yellow daisy-like flower, and yet it blooms practically all year round—simply because it wants to. Now, that's a happy-go-lucky plant!

The giant magnolia tree is blooming downtown. It is truly magnificent, with its big, pink, tulip-shaped, scented flowers. All week long, on my way to work, I'd stop at Dr. Insomnia's for coffee and sit under the magnolia tree for a couple of treasured moments at sunrise. Last night, after dinner, I took Bill over to the tree, and we stood under the streetlight smelling magnolia for about ten minutes. We couldn't get ourselves to leave. It was too wonderful.

This afternoon, Dad called. It's snowing in New York and it makes his heart hurt. His trip out here was postponed for health reasons, so now he's coming out at the end of the month. Then we will make arrangements together for the wedding. I still can't say the word *wedding*, but I can now write it, which is some improvement. I find it strange to be planning something so pure, that promises such happiness, when I'm still filled with such skepticism. Yesterday I drove out to some of the wineries and restaurants that do weddings. Some of them were too uppity and snooty and too expensive; others were too far away. Some were boring; some were just okay, but nothing special. I came home wiped out. I just don't know about this bride thing. It's beginning to make me feel very irritable.

MARCH 3

Today I drove out to Napa and Sonoma to look at more wedding places. The hills are so green and surrealistic. I played Bonnie Raitt tapes the whole way and sang—that was the best part of the whole day. Everything else got on my nerves. Everybody was so sugary. The minute they find out that you're the bride, they talk all gooey and chipper, and you just want to slap 'em. All I was there for was to see the space, find out the price, and get the hell out. By the end of the day my New Yorkness started leaking out of me, and now I feel bad if I offended anyone. They started asking about my dress and the bridesmaids' dresses—the theme? the colors?—and all that stuff I know nothing about. I don't ever *want* to know it. I'm just not a proper bride. I'm a dysfunctional bride whose relatives will probably be drinking, fighting, and rehashing the past during the ceremony.

Then they went on about "wedding etiquette": What is correct and what is traditional. I stood there with my mouth wide open. There is a whole wedding world out there. It's going on right under our noses and we don't even know it! I realized how many different kinds of women there are out there, and these wedding-planning ones are from a planet I never hope to visit. They told me I need fake nails and a pedicure before I get married! Why would I need a pedicure? Why would *anyone* need a pedicure? (These must be the women that Ma keeps telling me to be like.

Yesterday on the phone she told me I should stop being so independent and make Bill feel like I need him. She said I should stop all this nonsense about changing the world and women's rights. "Just hold on to Bill before someone else cops him!" I got off the phone and couldn't stop laughing!)

The bridal experts told me to pick up the latest issue of *Brides* magazine and to make sure and read, with my fiancé, the article on proper groom etiquette. Like Bill would actually ever read an article on groom etiquette. He'd just flip!!! Suddenly I was starting to feel dizzy. I found myself trapped in the Twilight Zone of Brides, and while I was trying to tiptoe out gracefully, I tripped on the stairs and they all came running to help me. Beautiful Stepford, bridal-know-it-all babes were surrounding me and squeaking as they walked me to my filthy Jeep.

MARCH 5

Last night a bunch of the crew went out for beers. I sat with the grips (of course) and listened to them whine about alimony and child support. The wife of one of the younger guys took his daughter away and won't let him see her and brainwashes the child to hate him. Now, I don't know the whole story, but I do know that a father should be allowed to see his own child. Unless, of course, he's abusive but in this case it's pure anger and resentment. I just don't get it. All these kids are having kids. They have no idea how to be good parents and then they go screw up the next generation. (If the world was run according to me . . . I would make it mandatory and easily available to receive some counseling before you are allowed to get a marriage license, before you parent a child, and before you could sign divorce papers. It's just too easy as it is right now and there's not enough thought going into these big decisions that take a lot of work, patience, and consideration.)

The ex-wife bashing was getting ugly and becoming political, so I changed the subject, sort of. I told them Bill and I were getting married. Everyone was happy and polite about it, saying "It's about time," even though most of them are in the middle of horrible divorce settlements. I felt like such a fool to have a drop of hope that maybe our relationship could beat the odds. I finished my half a Corona and waved goodbye. It was raining again and all the jerky drivers were out. I came home pissed off at the angry, divorced world, but when I walked in the door I saw that Bill had made a beautiful candlelit dinner—his famous Egg Belay dish, named after a climb. We sat under the skylight and listened to the rain. I asked him why we were getting married. Why we were doing something so stupid. What were we thinking? I confessed all my fears to him. Bill said, "Look, babe, we don't have to get married. Whatever you want to do is fine with me."

I got quiet for a while and thought about it. Then I said, "Ya know what? I really do want to marry you."

He said, "Great."

You see, he knows whatever he suggests, I'll choose the opposite. He was simply doing a Spy vs. Spy on me. But, I'm just one itttttty-bitty liiiitttlllle step ahead of him and I caught it in midair. Ha!

MARCH 10

I just got back from a shoot in Las Vegas. What a miserable place that is. Could there be any more desperate, chain-smoking losers than all those people on the strip? On the return trip I stopped in Los Angeles to see Sha. I planted three bougainvilleas and fifty gladiolas in her new little garden. She met a new guy and looks so happy; his name is Jim, and I think maybe he's the one. They were impressed with the little I know about gardening. It sounded like I knew what I was talking about, but if I'm so great, why is my garden such a bust?

The next day I took the train to San Diego to visit Ma and Ca. It was a beautiful ride until this weird, smiling guy sat next to me.

He watched me, and the minute I took my eyes off my book, he jumped right in and said, "Have you found Christ in your life yet?" I said, "No, thank you, I'm from New York." I quickly went back to reading and he didn't say another word. When we got to San Diego, Ca was there with one of her blond, beautiful, happy girlfriends. They were going out dancing, of course. They dropped me off at her house. I put on my Barbie pajamas and finished reading *Sweet Summer.*

The next day I went to visit Ma in her new apartment. She looked radiant. I always get scared that one day my parents will look really old and I'll have to deal with the fact that we're all growing up. But Ma still glowed and looked like my beautiful mother, so I didn't have to grow up yet after all and instead immediately regressed to age twelve. Just two days ago I was in charge of a fifty-man crew filming a night exterior, stunt/car chase down the Las Vegas strip. And right now, at this very moment, I'm in seventh grade and doing exactly what my mother tells me to. Right away she started in on me. Why do I call her at the wrong times? Why do I tell her what to eat? Why do I disagree with her? Why can't I just once say "Mommy, you're right"?

Next, Ca called, and Ma asked her big-shot-doctor-daughter to pick up a lemon, hair dye, shredded carrots, a powder puff, and a mop head.

We sat out in the sun and talked all afternoon. It was like the good old days. Ma pointed out people in her building and before she could finish her sentence we'd be laughing. Years ago, my mother and I would sit on the Madison Avenue bus making up stories about people; where they were from and where they were going. Were they winners or losers? Were they hiding secrets? She used to laugh all the time. This is the part that I miss most; life for her has become so hard and serious. We talked about the wedding. She insists on putting in money, even though I know she hardly has any. She said she's looking forward to it. I wanted to get on my knees and beg her not to fight with Daddy during the ceremony, but the words just wouldn't come out. I didn't want to ruin a perfectly good afternoon.

The last night was quite a fiasco. Ma is new in Southern California and doesn't quite get the concept of friendly, cheery, smiling, small-talking, healthy people. We were at the supermarket and the shallow, suntanned checker moved right into the danger zone by asking Ma where her accent was from. She basically told him it was none of his business and to stop being so nosy! All my childhood memories of my mother attacking nice, simple, innocent people came flashing in front of me. I was dying inside. I stood next to her as she told the checker that he should work faster and stop talking so much! I kept telling myself that someday this story would be funny, but that didn't stop me from feeling helpless and embarrassed. I took Ma to the car. We had a fight in the parking lot because I was so pissed off. I locked her in the car and went back inside the store to apologize to the checker. He looked as though he had just been hit by a tornado. I knew the feeling. When I went back outside, Ma looked so cute in the car that I felt sorry for her. It was the old, familiar, emotional roller coaster ride.

When I got home to Ca's house, Ca told me that food shopping with Ma is off limits for her. She has a reputation as a doctor in town. She doesn't want to be caught by one of her patients, in a supermarket hiding behind a magazine, cautiously peaking out behind the cereal display, pretending she doesn't know her own mother.

The next morning, Ma and I went to a flower market to get some wedding ideas. It was nothing great and made me miss home and the wonderful San Francisco flower market. We stopped at a café and had coffee. Ma told me new-old stories about her childhood. Recently she tried to speak to her mother about the beatings that went on in their house, and what a tyrant Saba was, but her mother still refuses to talk about it—pretends it never happened. It's just as Ma always said, "A camel never sees it's own hump."

Bill surprised me at the airport! There he was, standing at the gate with Bonnie Raitt's newest album. He talked even though he knows that I can't hear anything else when Bonnie sings. I wonder what he was talking about. I think it was about the water bill. We arrived home at sunset. The tulips were almost open! Yellow, purple, red, and orange—happy, healthy tulips. The jessamine vine was bursting with tiny, yellow blossoms, and all of the potato vines were going wild. Tons of little, yellow roses were blooming along the back fence. The African daisy was beginning to bloom in front of the fence. The forget-me-nots in the back were also standing up proudly. Spring is almost here, and it's even kinda here in our own backyard! It actually looks like we know what we're doing.

Go figure.

MARCH 12

I saw Liisa today. I felt like I had nothing to say and wasn't in the mood for her. I wore black. I told her about my visit to see my mother and that my father was coming out next week to help me plan the *W.* It was another rainy day, and I didn't want to look inward. I wanted instant satisfaction, like shopping or drugs or chocolate. She made me breathe; I got to lie down and close my eyes. That made me happy because a good nap can also be satisfying. When I sat up, I told Liisa that I had seen our home in Chicago from when I was five years old. My sisters and I were in our orange polka-dot, twirly, party dresses. We had our plastic celadon chairs and bright pink Hula Hoops out in the livingroom. We were sitting there with our favorite Barbie dolls on our laps, silently watching the two cute Chicago policemen question my mother and father. Someone had called the police because they heard a loud domestic dispute. Imagine that! My mother was screaming at them. She must have scared them away, because they left, looking a bit pale, without doing anything. After the show was over, we took our chairs and dolls and went to sleep. The next day, I bragged to everyone at school that we had real policemen at our house the night before.

They were all extremely jealous.

MARCH 13

A.M.   This month, Martha Stewart's calendar consists of training for her hike next month in India, breaking in new boots, making a list of new restaurants to try, and having her East Hampton lawn rolled and reseeded. That's after she plants the new vegetable garden, goes on-line, and appears on the *Today* show. Her life makes the rest of us look like a bunch of losers.

P.M.   I've been dog-sitting Cecily's dog, Patsy, for the last few days. She's a little black mutt from the pound. Maui and Max disappeared the whole time that Patsy was here—just ran away. Bill said it was important for them to see how good they have it. "Let them buy their own generic cat food and a warm cozy bed with flannel sheets. . . ." We were sad to lose Maui, but deep inside we were a little excited about the thought of losing Max. We've basically put up with him for the last year because we didn't want to return him to the Humane Society. They're very strict there. They make it hard enough to adopt anything in the first place. They almost wouldn't let our neighbor, New York Mike, adopt a dog, although they finally approved him. Now he drives around with his little, spoiled mutt, Pepper, in a car seat. The dog sits in a child's car seat and looks out the window like he's a prince. The Humane Society would be proud.

When I adopted Max, a woman from the Humane Society conducted a full interrogation about my life. I felt like I was at a job interview. I tried to impress her with all the famous people I work with, but she still wouldn't crack a smile. Just to adopt a lousy cat! She wanted to know that we'd be home all day long and wouldn't let the cat out of the house. I didn't tell her I worked twelve-hour days and that our last cat, Ebb, had been run over by our neighbor backing out of her garage. The neighbor was so horrified, she moved about three months later.

Well, this morning, after Patsy left, Maui came to the door but refused to come inside. She sat on the porch and peeked her head in the door every once in a while. I took food and water outside to her and we had a little chat. She's a little disappointed in us. This may take awhile for her to get over. I didn't realize she had such an issue with dogs.

I spent much of the morning digging spaces for my new brick border around the rose garden. When I came in for a break, big, grouchy Max was sitting on the porch bannister fuming. He's back and is *he* ever pissed! He wouldn't even look at me; he wouldn't come inside either. Maybe tonight they'll get over it and forgive us for putting such stress into their perfect little trivial lives.

I measured the border twice and figured I needed fifty scalloped bricks. I like to measure things with Bill's green fluorescent tape measure; it makes me feel like a grip. I also wanted to gain back some respect from Rich, across the street, after the lawn-mower incident. I saw him working in his yard and ran out front with my tape measure and looked real serious, like I was calculating monumental figures. Of course, it was obviously just a straight line, and he's a carpenter, so he probably wondered what the hell was taking me so long to figure out!

MARCH 14

On Sunday I fed all the roses with Epsom salt. I went around the yard and had a little chat with each rose as I poured the granules around each drip line. There must be twenty-five rosebushes! About half of them are miniature roses (I got a little carried away with the Jackson & Perkins catalog). If Bill knew there were twenty-five rosebushes around here, he would flip. He's too busy to count them, and I have them hidden next to other plants so they're not so obvious. If they ever bloom, I guess he'll realize that they all exist and that I'm compulsive and maybe he won't want to marry me after all. And all because of those Jackson & Perkins people. . . .

The extreme rains have brought more weeds. The weeds I hate the most are the ones that grow on top of the plastic or in between the cement sidewalk. They're so pushy. Don't they get it? They're obviously not wanted. I must have spent two hours out there weeding the front yard. Then I went to the landscape supply store and bought fifty more scalloped red bricks. It was quite a workout getting them into the car. Two cute young guys helped, but, of course, I had to make my point and lift as many bricks as each of them. I came home with a pain in my shoulder, but when I pulled in the driveway and saw our neighbor Rich across the street, I got my energy back. I figured if he saw me unloading fifty bricks into the wheelbarrow by myself, he'd respect me again and forget about the lawn-mower incident. I put on my cap, boots, and work gloves and began lifting bricks. The whole time I was out there suffering, he didn't even notice, until, of course, I was exhausted and dropped one of the bricks and it broke into three loud, earth-shattering pieces. He looked up from his car and I continued on, whistling as though nothing had happened. When he turned away, I ran inside to Bill and told him I was never leaving the house again. He told me that I'd never live down the lawn-mower-carburetor incident and that I should simply stop trying and forget about it. Then he told me that he was worried about me. He said I was turning into George Costanza.

MARCH 16

Ca called today. I told her I had seen the *Brady Bunch Movie* yesterday with some friends and we laughed louder than any of the kids in the theater. Ca acted cool and above it all, like she would never stoop that low and see the movie. But I was there with her in our childhood watching that program religiously. My sisters and I had a game. Whoever said 'ME' first about some TV show or movie won and you could be that actress for the day. For instance, I was Marlo Thomas in *That Girl* and Julie Andrews in *The Sound of Music.* I'm not proud, I can admit it. Obviously Ca has issues now because she chose Marsha. Marsha, Marsha, Marsha! That's not my problem.

MARCH 18

This morning the garden was very still. The sun was just coming up and I went out to throw some old lemons into the compost. Fatcat and her brown-and-white-striped, lazy friend were asleep on the picnic table. The friend ran, but Fatcat came over to the compost bin asking for attention. I kissed her and asked her again why she was so fat? She walked away, meowing. She's very sensitive and has an issue with weight. Maui watched from the kitchen window. She can be such a wimp. I went to look at my new border around the rose garden before the neighbors were awake and could catch me. It still looks like heaven, and I'm proud of my brickwork.

MARCH 20

This morning Bill dragged me out of bed to go for a nature walk along with Maui, Max, and Fatcat. It was one of the few clear days in weeks, and I guess they were all ready for a field trip! Bill walked around the entire yard pointing at plants and saying "Bust!" to any plant that wasn't blooming. "It's only March," I said, trying to reason with him. "Things will bloom in another month." But he was on a mission and nothing could stop him, until, that is, he reached the lilac tree. Last year it only put out one single, solitary, lilac blossom. The rest of the tree was just another bust. But today we found about thirty buds on it! Of course we don't believe they will ever open. But, that's another story. After the shock of the lilac blossoms, Bill discovered the America rose and the second Blaze rosebush on the less traveled side of the house! I heard him around the corner going, "B-A-A-A-B-E. . . ." I held my ground and stood tall. I told him that when all the magnificent roses bloom this summer, he'll wish that he'd had something to do with it. He rolled his eyes. He doesn't really believe that anything around here will ever bloom, because last year was just a tease. But, the older a garden, the better the garden. Young, new gardens are stark, one dimensional, and boring. They need time. They need some life, some growth, before they have anything to say. Before we had this garden, I was the most impatient person on earth (almost as bad as Sha!). If there's one thing you learn from waiting for a lousy flower to open, it's patience. You can still be cynical on the outside, but in your heart there has to be one single drop of hope for the flowers to hear.

Max left the nature walk early on because he found something much more interesting. He had a mouse, a poor little, helpless mouse. I chased him around the yard three times trying to save the half-alive mouse, but Max wouldn't give it up. Each time I got close, he'd grab it in his mouth and I'd hear little squeaky crying. I couldn't stand it and finally I ran inside to make coffee. Every few minutes the little mouse would fly up in the air outside the kitchen window. Max was pawing it and playing with it like it was a rubber toy. I couldn't stand it any longer. The only thing left to do was leave the house, so I went to make a bank deposit. The twenty-year-old yuppie bank teller was way too perky. As he did my transaction, he was singing to himself, with feeling, "Scoobie doobie do ba ba . . ." What the hell is *he* so happy about?

This added to my nausea from the cat and mouse chase. After doing three hours of errands, I got home and Max was still in the same spot with a stupid, possessive, proud smirk. I couldn't see the mouse and I didn't want to know what had happened to him.

MARCH 22

Last night the storm was fierce. I woke up every couple of hours and listened to the wind and buckets of raindrops, wondering if the skylight would start leaking. I was worried about my twenty precious yellow tulips that have just opened up, until Bill turned over and told me to watch out for the two redwood trees and to wake him up if they looked like they were headed for the house. Then, naturally, he fell back to sleep and I was up for good, my eyes wide open. My first thought was that we didn't have to worry about things like this in New York City! Maybe the smell of the subway stairwells wasn't so bad after all. I tossed and turned for hours, listening to the wild winds raging. At 4:45 A.M. I went to the kitchen and put some hot water on for tea. The electricity was out so I sat in candlelight. I meant to change our ancient gutters after the big storm last month but never got around to it, and now they were dumping water all in one spot — right on top of the honeysuckle that will never die. I sat at the table in Grandpa's flannel pajamas and thought about walking into the pouring rain like a crazy person, letting the water wash away all my fears. Instead, I sat in the kitchen and read about the spreading compost movement here in California. There are "master composters" out there. That sounds right up Bill's alley.

Suddenly it was light out. The rain had stopped. It was perfectly silent except for the leftover sounds of the chimes clashing in the wind and the one gutter pouring down water like a broken faucet over the honeysuckle. Morning had finally rolled around. I was so excited. I could finally wake up Bill and tell him that the redwood trees were still firmly rooted in the ground and that I had carefully watched them for the last hour and a half. Bill had all the windows in our room wide open! He says he likes to hear 'nature.' Maui was sleeping on his chest and Max (the mouse murderer) was snuggled up at his head, sharing the pillow like a true lover. I tried to slide in bed with all of them without bothering anyone. I put my head gently on Bill's pillow. Max growled at me and Maui wouldn't budge. They're so possessive.

MARCH 25

In the free-lance world there's an old saying that if you plan a vacation, you're sure to get work. It never fails—especially once you've bought your nonrefundable airline tickets. Well, I waited until a week before our vacation to Zion Park to purchase the tickets, and when I got home from the travel agency, there was a call on the answering machine for an original, artsy, nonviolent film project with a good budget and an eminent director. I was annoyed at the timing but I called the producer back. He asked if I was available for work next week, and I yelled, "No, because I have to go on a fucking vacation," and hung up before he could persuade me otherwise. It wasn't a very good first impression, and I wouldn't be surprised if he never calls me again. I put my raincoat back on and wandered around the backyard. It was raining lightly. I paced back and forth, pulled a few weeds, admired some early buds on rosebushes, and watched Max hiding around the corner of the shed, waiting to pounce on Maui's head. I tossed around the idea of ego—my big, fat ego that needs to be fed continuously. I wanted to take the job and was mad that we were going on vacation. But I was also torn because Bill and I hadn't had any real quality time together in weeks. I thought about Bill, and about what Grandpa Max told me years ago, about his forty-three-year marriage. When I was sixteen, I took a Greyhound bus to the west coast of Florida to a town called Naples, where the mineral baths are located. I just arrived one day at the pool, surprising Grandpa Max and Grandma Rose. Grandma had on her bright floral bathing suit, old sixties pointy sunglasses, and a green scarf around her head. She looked like a dream. They were shocked and practically had heart attacks at my surprise arrival. Even though I was wearing red lipstick, a halter top, and patched up, cut-off denim shorts, Grandpa still proudly introduced me to all the old biddies at the baths. That's how I knew how much Grandpa loved me.

I took a nice, long nap in the sun while Grandma poured half a bottle of baby oil on my back and kept saying, "So you don't burn." At sunset Grandpa gave me a driving lesson in his big, blue Cutlass. As we drove around the block a few times, he told me the secret to his marriage. "Annie-Panny," he said, "someday you will marry a nice Jewish boy, and the secret to a long marriage is taking a nice vacation from time to time . . . and a good coffee."

Shortly before Grandpa died, somewhere in his eighties, he was determined to renew his driver's license. He had to take the driving test three times until he finally passed. I spoke to him after each failed exam, and he rambled on about the driving instructors, blaming them and basically suggesting that there was a conspiracy at the Miami Department of Motor Vehicles to keep him off the road. I can't blame them. He drove like a turtle, and sometimes from behind you couldn't see his little round head and you'd swear his car was driving itself!

Bill came home in a bad mood, burned out from his busy life. I told him about the job offer. He said he absolutely needs a break and that if necessary he would go on the trip alone. Then he told my big, fat ego how great I am and that there'll be tons of work calls when I get home from Utah. He was just playing Spy vs. Spy on me, but I fell for it and I started getting excited about our trip next week. (By saying he'd go alone, he manipulated me into me saying I must go. He knows I'll choose the opposite of his suggestion.)

MARCH 27

Today, the camellia that I thought was dying, began blooming with beautiful, light pink flowers. I love camellias because they look like roses, only they grow in the shade and they're less needy; they're acid-loving plants. We planted a few of them between the redwood trees in the backyard. They grow tall, supposedly, and have an old English garden look to them. As I was standing there admiring my new camellia blossoms, Maui came out of the garage giving me dirty looks. She snubbed her new generic cat food that I had just bought on sale. She said I treated the flowers better than her and that one day she'd write a book about me. I felt bad so I mixed some of the old cat food with the new stuff and talked in a high-pitched squeaky voice, like when I talk to the roses, and she fell for it. She sat near me and ate her food like a good girl.

Once Maui was happy, I went off counting all the new buds in the garden. There were a lot. The Shasta daisy must have fifty! Most of the roses have at least five each, and the cineraria have about twenty each. Actually, the cineraria have had buds for the last few weeks, but we're starting to doubt that they will ever open — just like the bust rhododendrons. Once again, everyone said how easy cineraria is — a partial-shade perennial with beautiful purple flowers that bloom in early spring. Well, we've basically given up on the rhododendrons. I'm ready to pour an entire bag of acid fertilizer on them and run. But then Bill would ask me why I didn't read the directions.

When I finished bud counting, I packed the car up for my trip to visit Gwyneth in Santa Cruz. It was one of the few sunny days in weeks. I said goodbye to the cats and the garden and left Bill a long, mushy note. Before he left this morning, I stared at him extra long and hard just in case. This gets on his nerves but I don't care. It's the right thing to do before a road trip. My mother never let us leave the house angry. She made us kiss and make up. It's torture when you have to say you're sorry to your sister when you're still hating her guts.

I sang along with the radio all the way down Highway 1, belting out the blues like there was no tomorrow! It was a sunny Friday and I was free! I felt so lucky, like I was cutting school. Well, I never really cut school because I was a goody-goody, but I bet it felt like this. I stopped at Big Basin State Park and walked along the beach. An old couple were walking along the water holding hands and laughing. That's one of my dreams. It brought up the whole marriage thing to me and for the first time it didn't freak me out. I wanted it. I want to be with Bill for many, many years — through hundreds of laughs together; a couple dozen good crying breakdowns, a few more door slammings and walking away yelling "Fine," a thousand more mornings waking up to his face, and just a few more good arguments in the garden.

When I got to Santa Cruz, I parked the car near Bill's old office and watched the surfers. The first time I came to visit Bill, we parked the car in this very spot. It was his lunchbreak. It was raining and we sat in his fogged-in Dodge Dart and kissed for an hour and then ate soggy peanut butter sandwiches on the park bench. Bill pretends he doesn't remember this, but I know he does. Guys think they're too cool to be sentimental, but underneath layers of sports highlights, they're sweet.

When I got to Gwennie's house she was planting a Class Act rosebush. She had also just purchased an Amber Queen. I told her it looked like my Gypsy Dancer bush, and that sent us into hysterics. We used to be so cool. Out dancing, drinking, flirting, and all those other dangerous things, but now we sound like two old biddies comparing rosebushes with ridiculous names. I told her about planting with nitrogen now and about adding Epsom salts three weeks from now. I like to pretend I'm Martha Stewart, only Martha probably doesn't threaten her flowers to fucking bloom, or else.

Then we sat on the porch drinking peach tea and discussing the wedding, her husband Ken's amazing vegetable garden, and her art. I admired her painted clay pots. Gwennie's so talented, it makes me sick. I paint, but she's a painter. If I didn't love her so much, I'd be jealous. Well, actually, I *am* jealous. . . . We took a long walk around town, stopping at everyone's garden, and I showed off by knowing the names of all the flowers—*penstemon, campanula, rudbeckia, digitalis, coreopsis,* and *alstroemeria* just slipped off the tongue of this perfect little goody-goody.

After dinner, five-year-old Miles drew me a picture. He spent about half an hour on it and wouldn't let me see it until it was all done. Before I got a look at it, though, he began crying and tearing his art into pieces. He wouldn't let me comfort him. He sat in Gwyneth's lap and went on about how it didn't come out the way he had wanted it to. I sat there alone in the kitchen knowing exactly what he was going through. I still do that! I have tem-

per tantrums over most of my writing and almost all of my artwork. You see it in your mind one way and then it comes out completely different and you get frustrated and feel like a total loser.
Just last week I went on ranting and raving and tearing apart a
painting for my father that I had barely started. I ended up on
the couch sobbing in Bill's arms. I wonder if this is normal behavior for an adult. Miles is five years old; at least he has an excuse.

The next morning, I had breakfast with Bill's old friend, Charlie, before heading back north. Charlie has the perfect garden.
He's worked it for ten years and it stands proud. I could be jealous if I wanted to be, but I love him too much, plus he's generous with garden secrets and tips. We toured his yard. He gave
me some seedlings and asked me about the wedding. Everyone
is talking about the wedding. What did we talk about before this,
I wonder. Did we have a life?

MARCH 30

This morning at the bank, there was a man making a scene.
He looked crazy, but when he spoke, he was extremely knowl-
edgeable and articulate. There were about ten of us waiting on
line for the one teller, and there this guy was, reciting his consti-
tutional rights at the top of his voice. He kept saying "I demand
an explanation!" I'm not sure what he was talking about since I
came in too late and missed the beginning. The teller wasn't getting anywhere with him, so she finally called out her supervisor.
After ten minutes of wasting the supervisor's time, the man realized he wasn't getting anywhere and strutted off in a huff. As he
exited the bank, he turned back and yelled, "That's why I'm moving to the East Coast. I'm sick of this shit." Ha! I had to laugh!
Like the East Coast is any better? He doesn't have a clue what
he's in for! Good Luck Buddy!

April

April

APRIL 2

I finished packing for our trip. It was raining again, but that didn't stop me from going around to each plant to say goodbye for the week. Whenever I go away I like to look at them hard and long so that when I get back, I'll know what has grown or sprouted. When you look at them every single day, as I tend to do, it takes forever for things to change. This makes returning home from vacations sort of fun, instead of coming home depressed about getting back in your own rut. Bill came home from work, and I was out there with my raincoat on talking to the poor lemon tree. All this rain has made its leaves yellow; it desperately needs sunshine. When I return from Utah, I'll have to feed iron to the lemon tree, the camellia, and the hibiscus. The newest leaves are all yellow. If the old ones are yellow and the newest ones are green, it's a nitrogen deficiency. I feel bad leaving it in the middle of a storm. In fact, I feel worse about leaving the garden than the two cats.

On the windy, rainy plane ride to Utah, we talked about our honeymoon for the first time. We pulled out the map of the United States and pointed to places we'd like to visit. We both pointed to Alaska. I always wanted to go there. In high school, during my teenage depression, escape was on my mind and I thought Alaska would be remote enough for me not to be bothered by people. Of course, Bill wants to go to climb Mt. McKinley.

Right.

Like I want to climb a mountain on my honeymoon.

APRIL 5

Bryce Canyon was incredible. The sandstone is truly a natural wonder. Each day we hiked around for hours, far away from all the tourists and their bratty kids. We'd sit and have a picnic surrounded by the orange, red, and yellow wildflowers that were just beginning to bloom. No one has to threaten them. They just bloom on their own when they feel like it. What a concept. We stayed in the tiny town of Tropic, at Doug's Place. Doug must own everything. His name was on the town store, the laundromat, the post office, and the gift shop. I'd like to meet Doug.

Later camping out for a few nights it feels so good to stay at a hotel and have a warm shower. I was glad to get out of the campground and I'm sure the people at the campsite next to us are glad we're gone. I can just imagine them whispering about us, saying, "That young couple sure do bicker a lot." See, if you listen to Bill and me, you would think we can't stand each other. We absolutely love, love, love when the other one is wrong about something. We go on and on, shouting it from the rooftops! There is a whole ceremony performed over admitting that, God forbid, you were WRONG! Some recent examples might be forgetting keys, misplacing a wallet (his favorite), being late, choosing the item on the menu that turns out to be tastier, and singing the wrong words to a song on the radio. Last night Bill criticized the campfire that I built and I yelled at him for not putting enough water in the soup mix. This goes on for hours. Maybe everyone just needs someone to boss around.

Yesterday I decided that we should have a special day, once a week, when we don't answer each other sarcastically. It would be a day of peace, and we would have to be nice to each other no matter what. Well, we tried it today. As you can imagine, it was pure hell. Little digs would come slipping out and we had to retract nasty comments all day long. We kept apologizing, and taking back slanted comments. At the end of the day, we sat at the dinner table totally silent. It had been such a challenging day for us that we were left exhausted and speechless.

But tomorrow's another day, and we can go back to showing our true colors! I'm going to start the morning off with Bill's pinecone tossing contest. We see who can throw the farthest and hit the other one in the head while hiking down the canyon and pretending to be taking a picture, at the same time.

APRIL 6

Today was a cool, crispy, sunny day. We hiked around Zion Park for about six hours, then found a magical bed and breakfast in the town of Springdale. The owners have a spectacular garden and a white, fluffy kick-dog named Snow. Bill wasn't feeling well. I think the thought that our vacation was coming to an end and we'd have to return to real life, wiped him out. I brought down a pillow and a quilt and tucked him in on a lounge chair in the sun. Then I went investigating. The yard had every fruit tree imaginable, and all at least twenty years old! They were incredible. Tulips, geraniums, strawberries, lemon verbena, and climbing roses surrounded Bill as he slept at sunset with Snow on his lap and the rocks of Zion Park behind him. It all looked like a dream. I finished reading the book *A Thousand Acres,* just in time for the sky to get dark and cold. Then all the stars came out. It was magnificent. I still can't believe that all those stars are really light years away. It looks as though you can almost touch them. I kept hearing Carl Sagan going "billions and billions" in my head I thought about fighting with my sisters when I was eight years old because I said I could see the flag on the moon and they laughed at me.

Obviously they were jealous.

APRIL 10

We arrived home safely from our trip. The airline had overbooked and they ended up putting us in first class! We had Godiva chocolates and decaf lattes onboard. We pretended we were rich and famous, while we read about chicken manure in "Compost Corner" in this month's "ish" of *Organic Gardening.* (I absolutely love this magazine because of its editor, Mike McGrath. He refers to each issue as "ish" and his column is filled with words like this: "planted the #$@&*+# peas," or "I have no (bad word) idea how to plant this.") Reading his articles are kind of like listening to *Car Talk,* but this time it's about how to garden organically, and it is hysterical. They're all nuts, and somehow I have great respect and admiration for them.

When we got home, Maul and Max hardly noticed us. They simply went on with their useless, meaningless lives. Maul continued sleeping in the driveway with one eye half closed, and Max continued pawing an ant on the cement. That's why dogs are such far superior pets.

APRIL 11

Today was the first sunny day in a long time, warm like summer. Everyone seemed happy and shallow. Perfect weather for a visit to the nursery. I tricked myself into believing that I would go only to look. In about five minutes I was diving into my wallet, checking how much money I had on me. The columbines were blooming, and that's what got me started. They're one of Bill's favorite flowers. They looked like little wispy angels and pulled me into their spell. I regressed to my plant-shopping-obsessive-mode and went to get a cart. I don't ever take any of my friends with me to the nursery because they distract me. I like to be in my own little world, smelling flowers and reading what they're called and what they can do. I was pretty well behaved today. I walked away with three calla lilies, one ecchium, and one pink columbine.

When I got home, I sat under the pink jasmine and looked over the photos from the shoot last month. Gwyneth had sent me some pictures of us together on the set. She wrote a note saying, once again, that she was sick of being in pictures with me because I always had to hog up the whole frame and leave her in the background, basically nonexistent. I looked at the pictures again and saw her point. I didn't think that I looked good, but I sure looked important! I explained to her that since my sisters and I were seven years old it had been ingrained in us by our mother — the whole pose thing. With the Brownie camera glued to my mother's right eye, she'd command: "One foot out. Stand up straight. Stick your gigis out and try to look happy."

So today, when there's a camera around, we're like Pavlov's dogs. We hear the word *cheese* and we jump to attention and get that toe pointed in front of us. In one photo, Gwyneth was imitating me and she looked great. She stole the whole shot and left me in the dust. I'm so proud of her! When I finished staring at the pictures, trying to decide if I looked fat or not, I went around the garden counting how many tulips had actually bloomed. Not all of them had, and I felt gypped. I counted all the potential rosebuds that might open someday, but then again might not. Everything looked sort of hopeful except Ma's Peace rose. It sits there looking stubborn, like it isn't gonna budge. I don't expect everyone to be enthusiastic around here but it could at least show a little team spirit.

While I was out there surveying the land, one of our neighbors came by with a green bush and asked if I wanted an extra plant that he had. I asked him what it looks like when it blooms. He stared at me like I was crazy and said, "Ya know, Annie, not everything has to BLOOM." Then he turned and drove away with his boring, little, lonely bush sliding around in the back of his truck. I felt bad for the plant, but it doesn't bloom — it just stays green and that is simply unacceptable. Am I too set on a goal, a blossom, an ending? Must everything always be so productive?

Why can't I just enjoy a simple, plain green bush?

APRIL 12

This morning I turned down a big, long job because it was a project filled with car chases, killings, explosions, and crashes. I guess some people don't mind working on those kinds of movies. The studios make a ton of money, and the executives don't believe their movies have anything to do with promoting violence in a society that glorifies violence. To them, it's simply entertainment.

Well, they're a bunch of greedy liars.

This producer will probably tell everyone that I'm too ethical and I'll never work again.

APRIL 13

Today is Sunday. It's a sunny day with a delicate breeze that makes you feel good about the world. I woke Bill early so I could see his face. I can't help it. I love him like no one else on this planet, and every time I look into his eyes, I just can't get enough of him. He told me that if I wake him up again this early, just to look at him, he's going to start charging me.

I dragged him out of bed because it was the day we were to put in the vegetable garden, and I was excited. We had mango tea and semiburnt toast, and Bill did a perfect diagram, of course, of where we would plant everything. Max jumped up on the kitchen table and scratched Bill for no reason at all and ran. Bill threatened him again, telling Max he had one more chance and then it's back to the Humane Society. I watched poor Max cower in a corner near the bookcase. I don't know why I feel so sorry for him but I do. I would love to get rid of him but don't have the heart to do it. I put up with him, let him be a bully and have mood swings, and sometimes I love him, but most times not. I think I must have a codependent relationship with a cat.

While Bill finished his rocket scientist diagram, he made me read the directions on how to plant tomato plants. I HATE reading directions and he knows this, so he makes me do it just to torture me. See, you have to plant a tomato plant deeper than other vegetables. After removing the bottom leaflets you want to bury as much as half of the stem in the soil. Roots grow along the buried stem and make the plant grow strong. We finally got to go outside and begin planting. Last week I pulled out all the weeds and mixed in some general fertilizer. Yesterday we took shovels full of compost and mixed it into the wood planting boxes.

Last year the two of us fought the whole time about how to do things and where to plant what. But this year I didn't want to ruin his mood on planting day so I let him do it his way. It was actually kind of fun to relinquish control and just let Bill do what he wanted to do. I'm sure he's still wondering why I didn't argue with him out there. I'm sure he's suspicious and thinks I'm doing a Spy vs. Spy, but I'm not.

I just want peace.

We planted four tomato plants (Sweet 100, Early Girl, Big Boy, and Sugar Lump) in one box. Then we planted eggplant, peppers, and cucumbers in the other one. In the three smaller boxes, we planted two rows of strawberries, beets, lettuce, chard, basil, cilantro, chamomile, and rosemary. Along the fence, above the vegetables, we planted seeds of sunflowers, morning glories, hollyhocks, and beans. If everything comes up, it'll be a spectacular summer, but then, what's the chance of that happening? Today we feel optimistic, but who knows what tomorrow will bring. This is the first April we actually are a little pleased with what's blooming in the garden. Last year was a lot of work with nothing to show for it. It was more frustrating and depressing than anything. Things are starting to change around here. There's a shift beginning, and I can hardly believe it myself. We've been negative for so long, I don't know if we'll be able to stand ourselves being positive! I think underneath it, in some sick way, we enjoy walking around the yard saying to the plants, "Everything is bust," or "I hate everything," or "Just figures," or "Are you ever going to bloom?" or "What the hell is your *prob*lem?"

APRIL 15

Last night I picked up Dad at the airport. I was waiting nervously at the gate. We're going to spend a week together and I don't think we've ever done that before. For so many years he was always leaving us, and this time he was arriving to be with me. He was always too busy traveling for us to have real quality time together, and the few times we did have time alone together, I was still pissed off at him and the world. He came through the gate looking just like always, except without the business suit I was so accustomed to seeing him in. He was dressed in beige slacks, a sweatshirt, and sneakers. We had a teary moment, then he showed off his new rolling carry-on luggage as we cruised through the airport to the car. Once on the road, our first topic, of course, was food. We planned all our meals for the next seven days, and then there was a moment of silence as if we were suddenly exhausted.

Dad's excited about planning the wedding and is making me nervous! The whole drive home he was chattering away in his official work tone, scheduling my life for the next four months. I just want to hide, but he's making me deal with everything. He's excited and happy, and that makes me happy, even though I haven't slept all week. This wedding thing is keeping me awake and giving me nightmares. Sometimes I hear Bee Gee songs in my head at 3:00 A.M. What did I ever do to deserve that?

Dad fell asleep about halfway home. It was a rainy night and three little boys in the station wagon in front of us kept waving to me from the back window. It made me think of my sisters and all the idiotic car games we made up when we were skinny, toothless, little girls. We used to get so excited if someone actually waved back to us. When we were six, Daddy put a huge piece of plywood in the backseat, that became our bed at night and our drawing board during the day. For years, on long car trips, we drew our own masterpieces, wrote poetry, and played hangman and tic-tac-toe on it. It kept us quiet in the backseat so that my parents could argue uninterrupted in the front seat.

April

I watched my dad as he slept in the car and was thrilled to have him all to myself. No loud sisters to overshadow me and share him with. I felt so lucky to have him healthy and back in my life. He woke up when we went over the Golden Gate Bridge and admired the sparkling city in the delicate rain. He looked like a care-free tourist as he asked questions about all the towns on the map. We arrived home late. Bill was asleep. I kicked the cats off Dad's bed and tucked him in with his investment papers and Dean Ornish's book on heart disease. He looked all cozy in his pajamas — just like a kid.

I was up with the sun planting two six packs of hollyhocks in the front yard. When I came inside, Dad was on the kitchen phone checking on his investments. He seemed pleased with himself, so I guess it was a good day in stock land. We made decaf coffee and had a combination of three dry, bland, low-fat cereals. Dad had an itinerary written out of the four wedding sites we would look at in the wine country, and after breakfast we got right on the road. It was actually very comforting having him with me. Doing this stuff alone is frightening, but he made it fun. We stopped at every single stand along the country road for snacks, coffee, and fruit.

The first place we went to was an exclusive hotel in Napa. I walked in and wanted to turn around and walk right out. The woman was too snobby and her dress matched the floral design of the wallpaper. She really got on my nerves. I wanted to stick her to the wall and leave. Dad was polite and patient, of course . . . until she gave us the rates. They were astronomical and the room was dull and lifeless. She rattled off all the restrictions in her fake English accent, and I watched Dad try to get out of committing to anything. Once we were both safe inside the Jeep we burst out laughing. I can't believe that my Dad acts like this. He used to be so serious, now he's a blast. I felt like we were in high school together. He had me cracking up as he screeched out of the driveway, his nose turned up in the air, imitating the floral wallpaper lady.

We stopped at a vegetable stand on the side of the road and I

137

caught him trying to sneak a bag of pistachios without me seeing, hidden under the oranges and artichokes! I yelled at him in
front of the checker and made him put it back. I felt so mean, but
he's not supposed to be eating nuts. They're nothing but fat. We
got back in the car and he said that he couldn't wait to go visit
Ca because she isn't as strict with him. He kept shaking his head
and saying, "Yup, I can see this is going to be one tough week."

By the time we got to Sonoma, we were friends again. We
stopped at a café on the square and had tea and read the paper.
He read the business section and I read about a Marin County
woman who was put in prison for trying to flee the country with
her five-year-old daughter who was being sexually abused by her
father. The courts handed the girl to her father and jailed the
mother.

Is this a great judicial system or what?

We went to a nice restaurant in Sonoma that does weddings,
but it was already booked for practically the whole summer.
There was nothing left to do but have lunch. We went to an out-
door café with beautiful tulips on the patio. Dad was good. He
ordered pasta and I had a salad. We shared some merlot and took
pictures of each other and carried on about how grand life can
be. If only all days were like this—sunny day; driving around the
back roads; telling old stories, and new ones; eating out; stopping
to smell the roses; etc. We both felt blessed. I should've known
all this happy talk was leading up to him ordering dessert. He was
drooling over the dessert menu, asking about the strawberry
cheesecake, when I grabbed the menu out of his hand and told
the waiter to get lost if he wanted a tip.

On the way home we stopped at a couple of wineries with some
wedding potential, but by that point in the afternoon we were
both ready for a nap, so we called it a day. I put a cotton blanket
and pillow on the lounge chair under the plum tree and named
it Dad's Corner. While I was in the kitchen thinking up the next
boring, strictly low-fat, vegetarian meal for dinner, I watched him
from the window. Maui was napping on the picnic table above
him and Max was asleep at the end of his chair. They all looked

so content. I'm sure my father was dreaming about how to sneak out and buy himself a big fat steak and some Häagen-Dazs ice cream.

I kept staring out the kitchen window, hoping to lock in this picture of him, here at my house, before it became just another memory.

APRIL 17

A few years ago, Bill and I were out on a long bike ride and got lost in a little town called Nicasio. We had no idea where we were, but we loved it. We sat on the church steps and watched the cows and surrounding hills and thought that we had found heaven. The town consists of a red barn schoolhouse, a fire station, a general store, a restaurant, a church, a baseball diamond, a small real estate office, and I think that's it. I always suspected that I wanted to get married in Nicasio, but I wanted to see some other places before committing to it. Since Dad and I had looked at many other places and hadn't fallen in love with any of them, I decided to take him to my favorite one. I wasn't sure how he would feel about it, because it's such a remote place and he's used to big-city ambiance, but I think he got a kick out of it. We decided instantly that Nicasio was the place to have the wedding.

We walked around the restaurant and sat outside on the patio. It was a warm, sunny afternoon and the cows, horses, and chickens were out roaming around next door. The manager was pleasant and hip. She wasn't all frilly and didn't get on my nerves. She was wearing black so I liked her right away. We got down to business. We locked in the date and picked the menu. We told her that we'd come and have dinner on Friday night with Bill's mom to taste the food and go over the wine selection.

After we left the restaurant, we walked around the town. The wedding was slowly becoming a reality, although I was still basically in denial. Dad and I left Nicasio happy, our home-work done. There was nothing left to do but stop at Dr. Insomnia's to celebrate. I couldn't believe it, Dad tried to order a piece of pie!

When we arrived home, Max and Maui were waiting for Dad on his lounge chair. On the way out to his corner, he sneaked a couple of Coffee Nips from the kitchen cupboard. What's with him? Does he think I don't see these things?

I called Ca to give her an update. She was getting ready to go out dancing and couldn't really talk. She works long hours and then goes out dancing at night. Just listening to her life exhausts me! I went out to water the garden to recuperate from the phone call. I was thinking about Ca. When we were fifteen years old, Daddy bought us our first stereo system. It was delivered to our friend Sue's house a few blocks away, because her father, Alan, had arranged some kind of discount for us. That afternoon we sat in the lobby until dark, when Alan finally came home with three big boxes. It was a snowy December in New York City and freezing outside. All I remember is Ca and me sliding and pushing three heavy boxes through the storm, across 92nd Street, three blocks to our apartment building. Our wild dogs, Fluffy and Licorice, were barking and running behind us like maniacs. They were just as excited as we were. We kept falling in the snow and getting back up, laughing louder and louder. One of us would make it to the corner with one box and then come running back to help the other. The dogs had no idea what we were doing and didn't know who to stay with, and this drove them crazier and crazier. It was as if nothing else existed in the whole world except us, the barking dogs, the soft falling snow, the full moon, and our brand new record player.

I miss her. I miss our innocence.

APRIL 19

Yesterday it rained and rained and rained. It just wouldn't stop. I was going to feed the roses but now I'll wait and do that tomorrow. Dad came up with a new idea for teaching languages and we thought that we had a quick moneymaking scheme between us. Both of my parents speak about five languages, and we were going to make our own little dictionary. We started the one in Spanish. Dad got on the computer and began the concept. You see, this is what he does now that he's retired. His mind is still a workaholic's mind, but his body and heart say stop! Part of him is dying to jump back on the fast track. He must have been on the computer for three hours. Then he came into the kitchen with his pages and we took out all my art supplies and began designing a jacket cover. The two of us were sitting at the kitchen table, with the rain pouring down outside, drawing with crayons, cutting and pasting, and then laminating. We were both really focused on the work and were having fun. It was like being in an art class with your father, only he's a kid too. We made a big mess all afternoon and then decided that our idea wasn't so original after all, and probably wouldn't sell. So we both took a long nap.

After a long rainy day, Dad stayed in and Bill and I went to see the film *Dolores Claiborne,* based on my favorite Stephen King story. It was brilliant. I love stories about dysfunctional families, where women's friendships keep them alive. I cried through most of it. The mother-daughter relationship was too familiar to me. My eyes were red by the end, and I turned to Bill to ask him what he thought of it. He nonchalantly shrugged his shoulders as if he'd just watched a golf game and said it was okay.

They really are from Mars.

APRIL 20

Today was a fun day. The sun was shining early and the ranunculus bulbs are blooming—vibrant red, orange, yellow, and pink. I dragged Dad outside with me to do a nature walk and feed the roses. All of the roses have many buds on them, but few have actually bloomed yet. Patience, patience, patience. We packed up a lunch and headed toward Point Reyes. I took him to my favorite little beach. During the week, I usually have the beach to myself with a few joggers, dogs, or couples in love. I only take very special people there. Most of the time, my company consists of a blanket, a book, pretzels, and my Walkman. Today we brought a picnic basket filled with Caesar salad, pasta, a baguette, mineral water, and Coffee Nips. We sat down and ate immediately and then we took naps.

When we woke up, clouds had covered the sun, and it became windy and cold. We frantically began putting all of our San Francisco layers of sweaters back on, and then I began to cry. This whole wedding thing has made me a mess. I didn't want to cry in front of my father, but the tears just started falling. We sat there on the blanket, in the middle of a windstorm, and I told him how scared I was. I told him that since I was fifteen, I always wondered if both of my parents would be at my wedding and if they did show up, would they fight and humiliate me in public? Would Ma call him all those terrible names and then pick on us if we dared to defend him? Would he leave? Would I have to mediate the family's craziness on my wedding day?

We were quiet for a few minutes watching the waves and listening to the wind, as if it would give us the answers. It was uncomfortable, this topic always is. That's why we usually sweep it under the rug. Then he told me that he would stop in San Diego and have lunch alone with Ma. They would talk and plan how they could be civil to each other for one day. I can't believe he said this, I can't believe it's even possible. They haven't "had lunch" in about twenty years! This just doesn't happen in real life. I wonder if they can really pull this off? There's a major shift happening in our lives and I'm not quite sure if I trust it. The dreamer-idealist side of me wants to believe it can happen, but the minute Ma goes off firing expletives about Dad and his wife, it'll all be over and everyone will go back to their defensive, bitter, angry selves.

Oh, what's the use. . . .

APRIL 22

Last night was Daddy's last night in town. We went to dinner with Bill's mom, Virginia, at Rancho Nicasio. It was a warm Friday evening and you could smell the honeysuckle along the road. First we walked around the town admiring the Cecile Brunner climbing roses that looked as if they were as old as the town. Then we went in and ordered four different glasses of wine so that we could decide which ones to have at the reception. None of us drink very much and we were all quickly smashed. Dad and Virginia were busy telling old war stories. Bill and I had to order their food for them because they weren't paying attention.

The food was excellent. To celebrate Dad's last night in California, I let him have a skinny piece of cheesecake. He probably can't wait to get away from me! Virginia shared it with him. She's taking a step class in the morning. This woman is incredible. At sixty-something, after raising eight children on her own, she's out there jumping around at the gym, Rollerblading, and mountain biking. She's been through the deaths of her two husbands at a young age and she still has a positive outlook on life. She amazes me.

Daddy left that night after dinner, and Bill and I got home late to a dark, empty house. I looked in Dad's room. The bed was stripped. Everything was put away neatly. There was no clue that he had ever been here. I couldn't believe there were any tears left, but I found some more and I quietly cried myself to sleep.

APRIL 23

I woke up at 3:00 A.M. in a cold sweat. In my nightmare I was with my sisters and our childhood friend, Sue. We were seventeen again. We were tripping on acid. The sun was setting on a hot New York summer night and we were sitting on the steps of the Metropolitan Museum of Art, watching the windows "dance up and down" on the Fifth Avenue apartment buildings across the street. We were pointing and laughing, mesmerized. In the middle of our fun, the sky turned dark, and we were trapped in our bedroom. Ma was mad. She had just talked to Daddy on the phone and we detected a note of hostility in her voice. We deducted that it wasn't a pleasant conversation. Ma came into our room. She sat on my bed and cried, asking why he had left her and Ca and I tried to comfort her. Slowly but surely, she started calling him the usual names, so Ca and I ran to hide under my bed and cover our ears. We were tired of hearing what a sonofabitch our father was. In Ma's eyes he may have been a bad husband, but to us, he was our only father, and we loved him. Fluffy was hiding under the bed, growling. I had to shove him out of the way to make some room for us. How could he be thinking of himself at a time like this? Ma got louder and louder. Each sentence began with "Your father" and then continued on with every bad word you could possibly imagine in the English language. The windows in our room were wide open and any man hearing this on the streets of New York below us would certainly be running for his life by now. She was on her soapbox and, come hell or high water, nothing was going to stop her! Now, in an apartment building of well over a hundred people, you would think that at least one neighbor might find this uproar a little strange. Nope. No one ever came. That's what pissed me off the most.

Next dream, our room turned into Saba's barbershop. Ma was a young girl. She was on the floor crying. Her father was spinning in his barber chair laughing as he smoked a cigar. In this dream I was a grown-up and I was at work on a movie. I was having a bad day. I stormed into the barbershop set, waved my walkie-talkie antenna in front of Saba's scraggly face and yelled "You're so fucking fired!" Then I grabbed my mother off the floor, wiped off her tears, and saved her from him once and for all. I took her to the craft service table where we had a coffee and cake.

Then I woke up.

APRIL 25

I saw Liisa today. It was actually quite productive. I told her about all my dreams lately. She keeps telling me that this is all a normal process. Then I got to lie down and breathe. I love that part. Just like a nap! Lately I've been seeing prettier things. Like today, I was all alone in an ancient monastery somewhere in Europe, the sun was coming up and it was divine. I wasn't afraid—I was calm and content. I could see the sunlight slowly making its way through the windows.

May

MAY 3

Cineraria rocks! We planted three cinerarias in the shade garden last fall. They grew enormous green leaves for months. We were our usual skeptical selves and didn't think that they would ever bloom. But they did. They're stunning. Vibrant, rich, dark purple, and blue. Plus, the seed spread and we have about five more of them coming up in the side yard. They rate an A+. And we don't hand those out too loosely around here. Another surprise is the clematis. It has new growth! Clematis is an amazing plant. It looks like it's dying all winter long, its branches become bare and the wood looks dead. But then by mid-April it just pops back up out of its sleep and blooms enormous, spectacular flowers that look like they're made of colorful magic paper. Bill likes clematis so much that he hasn't added it to the list of restricted plants at the nursery.

After our garden survey, this morning at seven A.M., we did a snail hunt. This time, instead of the snail toss, we collected them all in a bucket and brought them over to a construction site a few blocks away and let them run wild. Tomorrow they'll probably be run over by a bulldozer! Maybe that'll teach them to stay outta my garden! They've eaten our hollyhocks and foxgloves and basically devoured our cucumber and eggplant. So I don't feel guilty.

I'm craving a nursery trip, but there's too much to do around here. I have to transplant the impatiens, feed the roses, plant new lettuce, and stake all the foxgloves in the front yard. I'd rather be floating slowly down the nursery aisles reading about new plants and seeing if anything more could possibly fit into our garden without Bill noticing.

MAY 7

This morning I was rummaging through some photo albums, trying to find a picture of me in the garden to send to Grandma with her Mother's Day card. I couldn't find one picture where the garden looked good. Figures. But I did come across the picture of the sisterhood in the orange sweaters.

About five years ago, while visiting Texas over the holidays, Ga bought matching sweaters for the sisters. She was living on a teacher's salary and found these horrendous, bright orange and yellow striped, polyester turtleneck sweaters on sale. She gave them to us on New Year's Eve. Because we love her, we were polite and thanked her without bursting into hysterical laughter. Of course, my mother thought they were beautiful and made us put them on and pose for a picture. All four of us in a row with loud orange stripes. Can you even imagine? "Gigis out, back straight, one foot forward, smile." *Flash.*

Over the years we broke the news to Ga, gently, that we thought the orange sweaters were hideous, but that we had found a purpose for them in our lives. They've become a highly sophisticated and subtle, yet strategic, torturing device. When you least expect it, —maybe on a birthday, maybe at Christmas, or simply as an "I miss you gift," —we send them to each other. The trick is to wrap the sweater in a fancy box or leave it in the trunk of a car or under a pillow after a family visit. We've come up with some great places over the last five years—and with only one sweater. Two sweaters mysteriously disappeared and one is still with Ga in Illinois. She says she wears it when she teaches, but I don't believe her.

MAY 14

Tomorrow is our birthday. Ca's and mine. I bought her the new Isabel Allende book and she got me the new Anne Tyler novel. Cecily, Gwyneth, Elissa, Ellen, and I were supposed to meet at Tennessee Valley Road for a birthday hike and picnic, but it was raining so we postponed it for a few days. I never really thought about it, but every year I throw my own little birthday party for myself. Does that mean I have great self-esteem or that I'm a total loser?

I hate when it rains on my birthday. Once, in New York City, it actually snowed on our birthday—in May! Ca and I were turning seventeen. We had just smoked pot at the bandshell in Central Park with Arf, Lief, and Mountain (you couldn't be a true Parkie unless you had a weird name). Since it was too cold to hang out at the park, we came home that afternoon and went on a mission. We were sick and tired of the cockroaches in the kitchen, so we sprayed Raid throughout all the cupboards. Well, every cockroach and his extended family came running out, frantically racing around the countertops. We attacked them with the vacuum cleaner. We swept them all up and then ran down the hallway together screaming, and threw them down the incinerator—like ladies, with our pinkies up! This went on for hours.

That's why I can't smoke pot anymore.

MAY 15

There's something to be said for Bill but at the moment I'm not sure what. My birthday gift was a climbing harness and a day pass at Class Five Fitness, a rock climbing gym. Well, it was basically a bust. I'm a lousy student and I talked back to Bill throughout the entire lesson. I just can't comprehend why anyone would want to climb a rock. Don't they have anything better to do? I had barely gotten off the ground when I began cursing Bill out for the next hour or two. He slowly and patiently taught me how to tie knots, how to belay, and how to rappel down the wall. I wasn't happy. I see now that I wasted so much energy in fear and in fighting with him that I wiped myself out early on. He finally lost his patience and said we were going home. He said I did fine for a beginner and that next week we would find some boulders that we could practice on outdoors. He was kind, but I think inside he was a little disappointed in me. He always thinks I can do anything. The only reason I want to climb again is because I'm mad at myself for not making it to the top and for being afraid. So now I have to do it.

That night, dressed up in layers of sweaters and hats, we climbed up lawn furniture to the roof of our house to watch the full moon. We sat side by side above our garden, which was actually showing some improvement. We could smell the jasmine and the honeysuckle. Bill told old climbing stories about the fingerbook and Mr. Louie. Many nights they slept on snowcapped mountain ledges in stormy weather. They had no money, no jobs, just some peanut butter and bread. They did this for years in their early twenties. In between climbing trips they would pick up some local work in whatever small country town they ended up in. Either carpentry work, painting houses, or pretending they knew what they were doing—like baking at Bru's Breads and Buns in Jackson Hole, Wyoming.

One of their clients in those days was Mr. Gifford, a wealthy realtor in Three Rivers, California. He paid them low wages to do all the worst odd jobs around his property. They couldn't stand him but they needed money for gas and food so they could head back to the mountains, their one and only love. After working on his land each day, they would go back to an old beaten-up one-room trailer they shared with two other climbers and called home. They had almost saved up enough money to skip town when Old Giff asked them to do two more projects. He told them he wanted two hundred feet of illegal pipeline covered up into the ground and his water tower painted. Burying the pipeline was the biggest pain. It was 95 degrees outside, and they had to cover it with rocks and pebbles and whatever else they could come up with in the dry, clay ground. On top of that, the wimpy kick-dog, Doggie Giff, would follow them every step of the way, barking and carrying on like he was protecting somebody. The sound of a couple of pebbles hitting the ground had Doggie Giff running for his life back to the main house.

The water tower was a five-minute walk from the main house. From Old Giff's window, he could barely see the top of it. Well, the painting team was getting bored with the two-day Rust-Oleum paint job and decided to only paint the front of the water tower, the side that Giff could see from his window. They knew that Old Giff was too lazy to do the uphill walk to the tower anytime soon. They had the old green Mercury Comet packed sky high with climbing gear, dirty clothes, and buckets of peanut butter, ready to roar out of town.

At 4:00 P.M. they went inside to collect their check from Giff. He was pleasant and didn't ask any questions; this concerned them a bit. Next, they went to the bank to cash their check. Mrs. Doggie Giff worked as a teller there. She went on about the expected heat wave, the local city council race, why boys grew their hair so long these days, and then slowly counted every single solitary dollar on the marble counter. They were sure this was a ploy. She was slowing them down and they figured Old Giff was on his way with his shotgun. Mr. Louie grabbed the cash and, as he lit a cigarette, winked and waved a final goodbye to Mrs. Giff. She giggled and waved back. Bill was in the car already, trying to start the Comet and praying that it didn't overheat again at this very minute. Just as they turned onto the highway south, leaving Three Rivers, they swear they saw Old Giff's gold Cadillac doing ninety miles an hour in hot pursuit, with little Doggie Giff barking hysterically in the front seat.

MAY 17

I was sitting under the jasmine, minding my own business in the backyard, when I came across an alarming article in the paper. It was about the religious right and abortion. It gave some statistics about how many millions of dollars they have spent over the last few years to fight a woman's right to choose. This was not a good way to start my day. Why are they wasting all this money? Why isn't it going to education, research, or contraception? Instead of putting so much energy and money into trying to control women, those who don't believe that abortion should be legal and available ought to be required to adopt and support one of the millions of unwanted children that are in our orphanages, hospitals, or living in poverty in the streets. Once all these children are loved, educated, and have proper homes and health care, then I'll believe that the pro-lifers are good, caring people and are really doing "God's work."

MAY 19

This morning I went around the yard at sunrise, scoping out the latest rosebud. I'm still waiting for the David Austin roses to bloom. I've been very patient, so they better be worth it. The three *rudbeckia* (black-eyed Susie) plants are starting to come up from under the ground. And this year they've doubled! All sorts of healthy green leaves are sprouting up around them. They're one of my favorites because they remind me of my cousin, Susie, and our old friend, Sue—both childhood allies.

I cut back the impatiens in the hanging basket on the porch. Impatiens are supposedly the number-one selling plant in America. I don't think they're *that* wonderful, but I guess it's because they're pretty undemanding. They're wonderful shade plants and look great near our fuchsias. You're supposed to be able to cut them back to six inches from the ground anytime during the growing season, and then two weeks later they're back with more flowers. Well, we'll see if that's really true. There's gotta be a catch.

I found a whole family of snails under the three outstanding foxgloves in the front yard. I tossed them into the street and decided to go on a serious snail hunt. While I accomplished this, I was thinking about the last time I visited Ca. She took the day off from work to be with me. We spent a whole day setting up a watering system, and planting a vegetable garden in her backyard and flowers in the front. It was hard work, but it felt so good to be close again. We started separating a bit when it sank in that I was getting married and supposedly growing up. She didn't express one single emotion, of course, but I felt it. Since I feel for both of us, I knew what was going on.

When we were done watering and planting, I helped her weed her new garden and taught her about snails, the enemy. She felt sorry for the snails and the weeds. She's a new, naive, innocent gardener. I felt so evil. Here I was teaching her to rip out all the so-called weeds and murder all the snails. I told her that once the snails started devouring her plants, she'd join the crusade. Then I told her that I might even be starting to like Scott, her young-stud boyfriend. I know that meant a lot to her because I had started out being so judgmental about their age difference. But I was only being protective because I love her.

I watched Ca weeding. Everything she does, she does perfectly. The section that she weeded was absolutely spotless. Not one little peep of a weed—all symmetrical. My section was a mess. As I watched her weed I was thinking back to when we were in high school. We were taking those horrid S.A.T. exams in New York City. It was early in the morning and Ca didn't have time for breakfast because she was always running late. Her stomach was growling loudly on the express train and we were both nervous wrecks. We ran the four long blocks to 10th Street, where the test was being given, and made it just on time. The intimidating examiner sat all thirty goody-goodies a seat apart and told us if anyone murmered so much as one word in the next three hours, we would be expelled immediately. Well, I guess Ca's stomach acids were churning from hunger and stress. Toward the middle of the three-hour exam, in the nervous silence, her stomach began growling so loud and long that it distracted the entire class. All thirty heads in the classroom turned to her and then immediately back to their exam. I just couldn't contain myself. I began laughing so hard that tears were flowing down my face. I was sitting behind Ca and I was praying that she didn't turn around, because if I saw her face I would be on the floor. Of course she turned around, just to torture me, and that threw me right over the edge. There was no turning back. We were laughing loud and strong with no end in sight. The scary examiner came over to us and threatened to throw us out. We both looked up at him in tears and agreed to be quiet.

But when he walked away from us, Ca's shoulders started shaking up and down again, and we simply couldn't stop laughing. We were out of control. He came over again, this time looking even more frightening. We begged him to let us stay and finish the exam. He finally compromised and put us on opposite ends of the room. Neither of us dared look at the other for the next two hours.

It was absolute torture.

After forty-two snails, I decided to hang up the snail hunt and went back on my garden walk. I was thinking about my sisters and how they make me laugh. There is a silent understanding among us because we survived a long dark period in our childhood together; we share secrets of a time too painful or too embarrassing to speak of. While other siblings were fighting with each other over schoolgirl nonsense, my sisters and I were busy being pillars of strength for one another to lean on.

MAY 20

Dahlia, dahlia, dahlia. Today my favorite flower in the whole wide world is the dahlia. I planted four of them in the spring—two yellow and two deep red cactus. Today some of the buds have opened into magnificent flowers. I really had my doubts when I was planting them because they are such strange bulbs. You'd never think they would turn into flowers.

After feeling proud of my dahlias, I did my delivery run for the food bank. In one of the apartments lived a single mom with five children. (Seventy-five percent of the poor in America are women. I think having five kids might have something to do with being poor.) The oldest girl, probably seven years old, was shy and hid behind her mother's dress. When I left, she opened up the curtains, knocked on the glass to get my attention, and waved. Her front teeth were missing and her smile broke my heart. She reminded me of myself at that age. I was *sooo* shy. I would never speak in class and I had no friends, because I didn't dare talk to anyone.

One day I came crying to my mother because Ca had so many friends and I had none. She rehearsed a script for me to use the next day in the PS 6 schoolyard, and I did it. I went up to a cute girl jumping rope alone. I asked her if she would be my friend; she said yes. Her name was Lashown. She asked me if I could skip. I shook my head, yes, even though I had only skipped rope with the lame white girls. We walked over to her other friends. They all cut dirty looks my way. Lashown yelled at them to give me a chance. They were playing double Dutch. Lashown and I were going to jump together while her other girlfriends turned the rope. I took a deep breath and jumped in. There must've been a sister up in heaven that day, because I made it almost all the way through "I like coffee, I like tea." Then the school bell rang and we had to stop. Lashown and I walked to class together, chewing gum and laughing.

I was in heaven.

The next year I became the teacher's pet and it got on Lashown's nerves, but she still stayed my friend. I don't know why. I was one big goody-two-shoes and smiled and laughed at all of Miss Heoxtor's jokes. I did my homework and did the extra credit assignments; I volunteered to be hall monitor. Oh . . . I was *pathetic!!* By sixth grade at PS 6, I finally made it into the cool-white-girl clique. I was torn between the homegirls and the white girls. The two groups didn't like each other so I shared my time between them. It wasn't easy, and I began to see that bigotry is taught to children when they're very young.

Each year, on the last day of school, Miss Heoxtor and I would exchange gifts. The last year I was becoming too cool and was embarrassed to be seen brownnosing with a teacher, so I rushed along to what had become our special little bench over the years, and quickly gave Miss Heoxtor the third makeup bag that my mother had bought for her, and she, with tears in her eyes, gave me a little, orange, patent leather handbag. I cherished my handbag and I cherished her, but I had to run off with the cool girls and pretend that I didn't care. I did a "girl" thing and joined Ca's clique because she had Josh Tager, Brian Lurie, Peter Solomon, and Rick Leach, and they were the cutest boys I had ever seen in my life. In fact, they were so cute that every time I got next to them I turned shy and lost my entire half-existent personality. I would stand there speechless. They were probably wondering how Ca's twin sister could be such a loser!

One afternoon in the schoolyard, Ca grabbed Brian's *Lost in Space* lunchbox and had all four boys chasing her! There she was, running around the PS 6 schoolyard with Josh, Brian, Peter, and Rick chasing her as if they were all in love with her. Just as I was about to burst with envy, she got hit in the eye with the lunchbox and had a black eye that lasted for two months.

Of course, she milked the injury and got all the attention at school and at home for weeks.

Figures.

MAY 22

A.M. Okay, everyone can sleep peacefully again. Ma's teakettle whistled! The teakettle I got her wasn't whistling, and, boy, did I hear about it. The whole world basically stopped. Well, she called me today to let me know that it now whistles loud and clear. She found this hysterical and was laughing her old great, howling, knee-slapping laugh.

P.M. Little Rebecca from next door came by this afternoon. Her kindergarten homework assignment was to walk in a garden, make a list of flowers, and draw three of them. She came over with her friend Derek. I got completely involved in her project, listing dozens of flower names, while she was off with Derek looking for insects in the compost pile. They were terribly disappointed because they didn't see any worms. Maybe our compost pile is a bust too.

Their favorite flowers were the nasturtium, foxglove, and godetia. I helped them draw the flowers in their notebooks. They asked why I had potato vine on every wall of the house. I told them it's because it's easy and it blooms. That shut them up. As usual, spending an hour with kids wiped me out, and when they left I was pleased to have peace and quiet again. I don't know how parents do it. My hormones tell me I want a baby, but my rational brain keeps looking at me and asking, Have you lost your *mind?*

MAY 23

It was a spectacular Saturday morning. No fog. The sun was shining in our window and it was already warm outside. Bill took off early for his Chinese medicine class, and I packed the car up with some snacks and my Rollerblades. First I drove up to Petaluma for a composting class. Later, I Rollerbladed around downtown, rocking to Annie Lennox and U2 on my Walkman. The compost class was given at the Sonoma County Landfill, and it consisted of me and a couple of old biddies. Sonoma Compost has a demonstration garden on the property. Tim, our instructor, walked us around the garden and showed us the different kinds of mulches and compost they produce on site. Their company converts yard trimmings such as grass, leaves, and brush, which were previously landfilled, and produces organic products for farmers, landscapers, and gardeners. It's a relatively new idea and definitely the wave of the future.

We saw three or four different types of compost bins and a lot of worms. We learned that you want 50 percent nitrogen, which means tossing in half green and half brown stuff. We learned about sandy and clay soils. If you have lots of sand in your soil, adding good mulch holds the water in. If you have clay soil, the mulch improves the drainage and makes oxygen available to the roots. Composted soil and mulch promote a healthy environment by adding thousands of microorganisms, essential nutrients, and organic matter to your bust soil at home.

At the end of the class, each student gets a complimentary bag of compost—sort of a party favor! Now, only a gardener would be excited to take home a bag of decomposed garbage. The soil was absolutely perfect. It didn't look anything like *our* compost. After all those hours of turning piles of dirt, we still have a box of big clumps and twigs, and it's never ever at the correct temperature.

Boy, will Bill be jealous when he sees this!

I'll have to show it to him gently or he'll break. I tell ya, he'll break!

On the way home I stopped off at the International House of Pancakes. Have you been in one of those lately? They're filled with martians! Since we don't eat a lot of eggs, I asked them to please save me all their eggshells and I would pick them up tomorrow. Bill read that a line of crushed eggshells along the vegetable box will cut snails. The martians were very friendly and didn't look at me like there was something wrong with me. In fact, they were all interested in my experiment and the outcome. (I think they were just excited to have a customer from the planet Earth.) All we need is a few innocent snail victims to pass our eggshell barricade and we're all set! They'll be running off telling all their loser snail friends "Yo, I've been cut, man. Let's get outta here!"

MAY 25

Today Cecily and I went to hear Gloria Steinem speak at Book Passage, and the store was packed. Gloria was brilliantly powerful and vulnerable at the same time. It made me like her even more. She sent out a message of strength and hope for the future and even cracked a few jokes. When I got home that evening, the book that I'd gotten in the mail from a friend, called *Wedding Etiquette* (you know, the one with the perfect bride on it), was on the kitchen table. I had written in heavy black marker GET A FUCKING LIFE across the front of it because I was in shock that such a book seriously existed. Well, it just so happens that Bill's mom had stopped by to drop off some mail for him. Bill was sitting at home alone, making his own dinner. As his Mom held the violated etiquette book in her hands, she asked where I was? Bill told her that I wasn't at home because I was at a feminist rally with Gloria Steinem.

Oy!

June

June

JUNE 1

Summer is here and it is hot! I spent three laborious hours in the garden today. I was trying to avoid making a guest list for the wedding. The minute I sit down and make that list, it all becomes a reality, and I just can't face it. So, instead, I tore up the garden. I hunted out every single weed and snail and dragged them outta here. Then I went around hunting for pests and diseases. I fed iron to some yellowing plants and staked up the gladiolas, which have just begun to bloom. I transplanted the ivy geranium and lemon rose geranium into bigger pots. Geraniums are becoming some of my favorite plants because they're so easy, and they bloom! I weed-wacked the front yard from head to toe. You gotta love the weed wacker! I mean, just saying the name is a blast! I planted amaranth for Bill. It's his favorite lettuce, it's easy to grow, and it has beautiful reddish-purple leaves. I planted it in between the sunflowers and the tomatoes that are now about three feet high. Everything is really starting to grow and blossom in our garden. We don't know what we did to deserve this, but we're sure there's got to be a catch.

Yesterday we picked out the invitations. Of course they have a floral design on them. Talk about obsessed. I guess we have a flower issue. After I ran out of things to do in the garden, I came in, made a cup of ice coffee, and started making the list. It was stressful but fun at the same time. I was thinking about my parents. They met a few weeks ago to discuss the wedding plans. They went out to lunch and they were civil. This is a good sign.

JUNE 3

I saw Liisa today. I had just finished reading *The Tibetan Book of Living and Dying* and we talked about Tibet. I remember when I was twenty and visiting my dad in Belgium, we watched a program on the Tibetan monks. They were sitting on mountaintops and praying for hours. I was so moved by this. I wanted to leave my life and become one of them. But, then I got a call to be the tenth parking p.a. on my first movie, *Staying Alive*, and I went back to New York to become a workaholic instead. My first lowly job position required me to sit up all night long, in the West Village, watching picture cars, guarding parking spaces, and speaking on walkie-talkie to the other nine loser parking p.a.'s. I did this with such flare that a week later I got a call to be the assistant to the Craft Service person on a Robin Williams movie. Here I basically shlepped bagels and coffee and picked up garbage. The only plus of the job was bringing breakfast to Robin's trailer every morning and shooting the breeze with him. After all the egomaniacs I've worked with over the years, he still stands out as one of the few modest and decent people in the film business. I showed such initiative at such menial tasks that a week later I was moved up to a real live Production Assistant on the set. Here I woke up at four o'clock each morning, ran around like crazy for thirteen to sixteen hours, got bossed around by lots of highly affected and pompous lunatics, returned home at nine P.M., walked up three flights of stairs with thirty walkie-talkies to charge overnight, and made seventy dollars a day. Ain't no glamour here. No sirree.

JUNE 4

If you asked me today what my favorite plant is, I would have to say lavatera. It's bursting with a million deep dark pink wispy flowers. You can buy a one gallon plant and in one year it grows to a four to five-foot beautiful bush that blooms all summer long. We have three already and I want to buy more of them, but then

I'd look obsessed, and I'm trying to clean up my image. I fed the new snapdragons and cosmos with fish fertilizer. Maui was licking the fertilizer bottle, and then she came over and rubbed her little, furry face against my cheek and I almost fainted from her breath. Next I moved the clay birdbath a few inches over so that the Peruvian lily, another prolific plant, would have more room to grow. I picked up the top basin and under it were fifty gross earwigs zipping around. So, of course, I flashed back to New York cockroaches and started screaming and running for my life. Such spineless behavior would certainly disqualify me as a master gardener.

JUNE 5

This afternoon I met Pucci on Fillmore street. We started the wedding dress hunt. Thank God she was interested in it, because I would've blocked it out for a few more months. And she had all these ideas of where to shop and how to look. Elissa had told me that Betsey Johnson had some white lace dresses in the window when she passed by last week. Well, Betsey Johnson is a little too cool for me, but I thought we'd check it out anyway, because I know Elissa has good taste. So that was our first stop. I tried on some pure, sweet, white dresses, but I felt too cutesy, and it wasn't me. Then we found it! Pucci and I fell in love with it immediately! It's not really a dress. I'm not sure what you call it. It's a tight, white, lacy one-piece bodysuit with baggy, lacy pants. It's wild—sexy, yet smart and powerful. I love it. I wasn't sure if I had the nerve to wear it, but Pucci said I had to, because it makes a statement and it's me. You see, that's why girlfriends are so important—they make you remember who you are. I stopped by Elissa's house on the way home to show her my wedding dress. She said, "That's not a dress. That's a wedding-a-go-go outfit."

So that's what we call it.

JUNE 6

When Bill came home at sunset, we sat together in each other's arms and admired all the roses. The world finally slowed down for a few minutes. I pointed to each rosebush and told him the pros and cons of each rose. He was wearing his purple T-shirt that always makes me fall in love with him all over again. I asked him once more if he really, really wanted to get married? He looked at me and rolled his eyes. Then he sang me the song he sings to Maui, very much off key, "You're my little bumpkin and I love you so. . . ."

JUNE 11

The first flower on the black-eyed Susie bloomed today in honor of Sha's birthday. It brought back memories of playing Monopoly with her when we were kids. It took Ca and me about three years to figure out that because she always made herself the banker she always won! Actually, if there were an award for the best big sister, Sha would win it hands down. She's always been there when I needed her, ready to lend support or give a pep talk. Years ago, when I left New York, I stayed with her for a few weeks in Los Angeles. It was the first time I had worked on a Hollywood stage and I was scared to death. The day I started work, she drove me to the Warner Brothers lot at seven in the morning. I was too scared to speak, so she gave my name to the guard at the gate, as if I was someone important and he should be impressed, and then she drove me to the stage door. I couldn't get out of the car. I was petrified. I just wanted to turn right around and go home. In the middle of my whining, she literally pushed me out of the passenger seat, threw my bag to me, locked the doors, and yelled, "You get the hell in there and show them what you're made of!" Then she screeched away, almost running over the wardrobe lady, and I went inside believing I was great because my big sister said so.

June

JUNE 12

This afternoon I told Ma that we were having a rabbi and a priest at our wedding so that both mothers would be pleased, and both religions fulfilled. Well, I didn't expect such a stunning response. She was very upset, to say the least. She said that it would be extremely difficult to find a priest and rabbi willing to do a joint ceremony. Since I know nothing about religion, I didn't have a clue. Aren't these the people telling everyone to love everyone else? When push comes to shove, where is the tolerance they preach?

Anyway, the good thing about this is, it motivated my mother to call my father and they had a discussion. Yay! Ten minutes later, my father called me. Speaking in his serious, fatherly tone, he told me that Grandpa would not have approved of having a priest at my wedding. Now, I can appreciate his wanting to protect our Jewish identity especially after surviving the Holocaust, but I also believe that if we stay segregated, we're allowing the same mentality of close-minded racists to do the same thing all over again. So Dad and I got into a whole ethical debate that went on and on and on. I told him that I couldn't care less if any type of structured religious person was performing our ceremony and that we were only doing it to make our parents happy. I just don't get this religion thing. To me it seems so hypocritical. It may have started out as a good thing, but throughout history and still today it continues to divide people, start a lot of unnecessary wars, and globally breed a bunch of extremist wackos. This got poor Dad in a tizzy! I felt bad, guilty. I let out a gigantic sigh, and told him I'd discuss it with Bill and we'd call him back later.

When Bill got home I brought the subject up. He reminded me that he was an altar boy for three years. Talk about a goody-goody! Then he called his friend Charlie in Santa Cruz. Charlie has some kind of minister's license you can get in the mail or off a cereal box or something. Charlie was honored and gladly accepted the job of marrying us. I called back each of my parents that night and told them there would be no priest and no rabbi. Our friend Charlie would perform the ceremony. He's a gay chiropractor, acupuncturist, Buddhist minister who lives near the beach.

I must've exhausted them because they were fine with that. Go figure.

JUNE 13

The black-eyed Susies are bursting with flowers. They are such happy plants—it's like they're smiling at you all day long. In a few days it will be Father's Day. I painted Daddy a flower pot and wrote him a mushy, gushy, goody-two-shoes card. Tears started falling while I wrote to him. All this stuff from the past has been coming up, and I just want to sweep it back under the carpet. I wish I could be like all those people who can do that with their childhoods, but no, not me. I have to remember every single, excruciating moment and then, of course, I must analyze it to death. I decided to call him, for no reason but just because I could. When he heard my voice, he sounded so excited to hear from me that I melted. He was making his famous salad dressing and a low-fat lunch. There was a heat wave in New York, so he was staying in his air-conditioned apartment and writing his memories of the Holocaust. I told him that no matter what I do, my salad dressing never tastes as good as his, and that my chicken soup never tastes as great as Ma's. He said, "Annie, that's all emotional. You're just holding on to the past." I hung up the phone and started wondering why I was holding on so tight. There was so much good stuff mixed in with the bad. That's what makes it so difficult. Life just isn't crispy clear, black and white. It's all so complex.

JUNE 14

Godetia, godetia, godetia. Have I talked about godetias yet? Godetias are part of the clarkia family and they are outstanding summer-blooming annuals. They are one of the few annuals I even allow around here, and they deserve bonus points. One six-pack brought us six showy small bushes of light pink and dark magenta flowers. Plus, they are excellent cut flowers. Any friend who comes over has to be dragged around to see all the godetias and hear my story about how I bought them by accident last year.

Another very different plant, but also one of my latest favorites, is hydrangea. We have a few lace-cap hydrangeas in the backyard. They do great in partial shade and have big, lacy, white flower clusters all summer long. This is the first year that they bloomed, and they are incredible. Supposedly you can change the color of the pink hydrangeas to blue by adding aluminum sulfate to the soil. Bill says the blue hydrangeas remind him of old ladies with blue hair and doesn't understand how anyone could think that's attractive. He may have a point.

After admiring the godetias and the hydrangeas and taking full credit for them, I went to check up on the echinaceas. Last year the snails ate most of the young echinaceas, but now we have a mixture of grapefruit rinds, beer, and eggshells all around the flowers, so the snails can choose their own torture or get the hell out of the garden. So far it's working, and even the new echinaceas are surviving. Echinacea, purple coneflower, is definitely on the top ten list. They're simple and relatively undemanding plants, which is what we like around here. They grow three-four feet tall and have beautiful, deep purple, drooping rays around a dark center. They bloom in summer for a long time and are one of Bill's favorite flowers.

What have I become?

JUNE 17

This week, while on location in Healdsburg, I was peer-pressured by the grip department to smoke some "pot-lite," and twenty minutes later I was attacked by a giant bug. It was sunset and I had just arrived at the hotel and taken a shower. I went back downstairs to get my makeup bag (I know, I can't believe I have one either). I was wearing a T-shirt, shorts, and I was barefoot. In the parking lot I stepped on the most enormous cockroach I have ever seen in my entire life — probably five inches long, and it had wings! My foot had accidentally turned him over on his back and he was stuck there waving his legs in the air and crying for help. I ran for my life, to my car, repeating to myself, "That didn't really happen, that didn't really happen, that didn't really happen."

See? I told you I can't smoke pot anymore.

JUNE 20

My friend Barbara is visiting from Colorado. She arrived just in time to help me plant the drought-tolerant section! She was barely out of her car before I had her digging holes in the hot sun.

So here was Barbara telling me laborious road stories while we planted liatris, three colors of yarrow, false heather, echium, salvia, pincushions, and wallflowers. Then we had a dump truck deliver wood chips and spent another hour and a half spreading them around the plants. By sunset we were wiped out, and if Barbara hadn't been so exhausted she probably would've split town, afraid that if she stayed I might make her do another garden project the next day. It's been known to happen. She claims that after visits with me, she always needs a vacation.

The next morning I let her sleep in. But the minute she opened an eye, I went in there and told her to get dressed for the nature walk through the garden. Ca calls our house the Discovery Channel. I take it as a compliment, but I think she thinks we're a couple of nerds. It was cloudy and damp outside, but the flowers looked beautiful. The butterfly bush was blooming. It's supposed to attract butterflies! Barbara's an ex–New Yorker too, so of course she asked if any "fucking butterflies ever come around." Then she tried to make me nervous by counting the days until the wedding. I've basically blocked it all out. The only panic I feel is in my dreams, so lately I've been having insomnia. We made peach tea and sat near the striking red salvia. We laughed about the old times together dating jerks. She saved me at many wrap parties. One and half beers and I was out of control. I'd be dancing on tables with wild, gorgeous grips who she knew would simply tear my heart out. She'd come out in the middle of the dance floor, put her emerald ring on my finger, tell the guy I was engaged, and drag me out of there. That's true friendship. We talked about the guy she was seeing. It didn't work out. He's a professional rock climber. He gave her an expensive harness, shoes, and rope, and taught her how to climb; and then when she got too close, he went running as if he'd seen a ghost!

Later that day we went Rollerblading. Barbara's much better than I am, especially on the hills. She was leading, and somehow we kept ending up on hills. She was probably paying me back for making her work so hard in the garden yesterday. When we got home, I went outside to turn on the drip system and saw a beautiful butterfly on the butterfly bush! I called Barbara, but by the time she came out, it had disappeared, and now she doesn't believe me.

Figures.

JUNE 23

This morning a package arrived for us from Tiffany's. It was a beautiful flower vase sent to us from family in New York—our first wedding present. Maybe this wedding thing isn't so bad after all. Maybe I was looking at it all wrong. . . .

JUNE 24

Today was the longest day of the year. At 9:00 P.M. it was still sunny and hot outside. I picked up a six-pack of sunflowers today. Bill and I got into a fight about where to plant them and

I slammed the door and strutted off like I was hot stuff. I don't know why people have to fight about the dumbest things. I walked around the neighborhood for half an hour, angry, hoping that he was worrying about me. But when I got home he was sitting on the couch reading the sports page, looking like he didn't have a care in the world. I wanted to scream and throw things about and carry on all out of control, but that's not in my nature, so I just put on my pajamas, tucked myself in bed, and prayed that I would fall asleep. Bill came in and had no clue that we were even in a fight! What planet are they from? After I said nothing was wrong about three times, he finally dragged it out of me. I had tears in my eyes. Why does it take tears to make men listen?

I just wasn't happy with how our relationship was going and I was starting to build resentment—BLAME and RESENTMENT. Those are the culprits. Once the seeds are sown, you can't let them grow. You have to nip them in the bud or else it gets harder and harder to hear each other. So we talked for about two hours—talked about how a good marriage is work and how it needs care and attention. I was so proud of myself, because I didn't apologize for what I was feeling. I simply expressed my-self. Women are so used to saying "I'm sorry" all the time. What the fuck are we so sorry about?

I felt that we've both been busy in our own little worlds the last few weeks, instead of making time to be close. Plus the thought of the wedding soon makes us moody. We need to get away from our lives and remember all the true reasons why we fell in love with each other in the first place. I guess I did most of the talk-ing. I felt so much better afterward. I could breathe again. I think Bill was only happy to see me happy and to be off my shit list.

Men are less complex.
A baseball game would've done just as well.

JUNE 25

Oh, it's just no use. We can't hide it any longer, we're definitely obsessed. I walked up the driveway to our house. Blooming flowers surrounded the yard. Cut flowers were in vases in every single room of the house and the flower vases have painted flowers on them. People must walk into our house and want to throw up.

It hit 99 degrees today. All the flowers were drooping and suffering. I went around in a panic turning on all the drip systems, and soaking as many plants as possible with the hose. Then I found myself staking up more and more flowers. I was yelling at them to stand up straight. I felt like my mother. That didn't stop me though, and it concerns me a little. I watered the new daylily—a possible bust plant, but the jury's still out. At least it's said to be tough and disease resistant. Bill bought it a couple days ago while on a spending spree. Thank God he got it instead of me or else I'd never hear the end of it. I guess the flowers only last for one day, and then you have to snap them off so more will bloom. Just what we need, more work.

Last night we sat down and addressed all the wedding invitations. It took hours and it wasn't really that much fun. When you have a certain budget, you can't invite everyone and that makes it hard. It's difficult deciding who to invite. Only your family and closest friends? Or all your work friends, your boss, rich friends, influential friends, and the ones you know won't make it but will send you a big expensive gift? We included that last group.

JUNE 26

This morning, on the way in to work, I stopped at the mailbox, took a deep breath and quickly tossed the wedding invitations in. This is it—no turning back now. The heat wave took my mind right off the invitations. I was worrying about the garden and how I wanted to be home all day, watering the flowers every couple of hours. Now if that's not obsessive, I don't know what is. I got to the set and the first person I saw was Sandy, the grip. Last week he stopped by our house to drop off some equipment for work. I wasn't home so I left him the key. This morning when he saw me, he said, "Your house is beautiful, almost perfect. Lots of flowers. Lots and lots and *lots* of flowers. Thank God you had dirty dishes in the sink or I would've been afraid—very afraid."

And then he walked away.

JUNE 27

Today is Bill's birthday. I treasure the day that he was born. This morning, as the sun broke through the blinds and onto his beautiful face, I watched him sleep on the pale yellow sheets. He's perfect to me. He's handsome, brilliant, kind, and he has no body fat. He tells me it's rude to stare, but I can't help it because I'm madly in love with him and each year it's deeper and deeper.

Mr. Louie gave Bill a splendid gift, the Hydroblaster! It's a gigantic water gun that can squirt real far. At 7:30 this morning Bill was hiding behind the cat door waiting for Max to come clumsily pouncing through like he owns the whole world. Instead, better prey arrived. Fatcat and psycho kitty came tiptoeing around the deck looking for free food. Bill was armed and ready with his Hydroblaster and blasted them right over the fence. Max must've heard the commotion and the poor thing had to get off our cozy bed and walk a few feet to see what was going on. I guess he hadn't learned about the Hydroblaster in kitty juvenile delinquent school! He walked right past Bill with his snitty little nose and tail in the air, and onto the deck.

ZZZZAAAPPP!!!

Bill BLASTED him until there was no water left in the neon plastic tank. After rolling around laughing on the garage floor, we looked up, and Maui was sitting in the kitchen window, right near the phone, watching us in disgust.

She probably had just reported us to the Humane Society.

JUNE 29

Last night I couldn't fall asleep. Maybe it was the ice coffee I had in the afternoon with Elissa or maybe it was because I was thinking about the wedding. The invitations are out, so that kind of makes things official, doesn't it? No turning back now. Well, the little insomnia people that sit around laughing at you in the middle of the night had me but good. I tossed and turned for a while, but I didn't give in; never once did I look at the clock. In fact, I tried a Spy vs. Spy and kept telling myself how glad I was to be wide awake in the middle of the night and how productive a time I was making of it. But I think Spy vs. Spy only works well with your mate, not with yourself. Just to make matters worse, on top of all the noise going on in my head, there was a bird fest going on in the backyard. I swear every single neighborhood bird and its entire family came to party in the apple tree right outside our bedroom window. I guess it was a midnight jam session, because each bird whistled a different annoying, whiny tune at the top of its little bird lungs. Just when I thought I couldn't take it anymore, a little lightbulb went off in my exhausted head and I jumped out of bed with a mission.

The Hydroblaster!!

I filled it up at the kitchen sink and then proceeded cautiously into the night. I got to the tree and threatened that I would call the police, but that didn't faze them one iota. They just kept rocking their little melodies like I didn't even exist. So there was nothing left to do but blast the apple tree like there was no tomorrow.

Then there was silence.

I waited out on the deck for five minutes to make sure they took all their friends with them and left for good, then I tiptoed back into the house. I passed Maui sleeping on the sofa. Thank God she didn't wake up; I couldn't take any more of her self-righteous looks. I got back in bed and just as my head hit the pillow, I heard a few slow, staccato chirps. It was the bird leader, back with the hard-core night owls, and gradually their chirping rose to a crescendo, and it was just basically a nightmare and there was nothing I could do about it. I don't remember when I fell asleep, but I do know that first thing this morning I heard the same irritating birds chirping outside the window, whistling a happy-go-lucky little morning melody. My first thought was to run outside and choke their skinny little necks, but I was too tired to get out of bed.

JUNE 30

Today I bought a flowery (what else?), flowing yellow dress with orange flowers and celadon leaves. It's for the bridal shower that Cecily is making me have. It's almost a bit too chipper, but I'm trying to get away from wearing black and expecting doom. If I want to regress to being cynical, all I have to do is have a conversation with Bill. He gets concerned when I get too positive. The only reason he talked to me at that party we met at seven years ago was because I was wearing a morbid black dress in the middle of a beautiful sunny day, and I was bitching about how unfair the world is and what's the point of going on? He came running over and asked for my number.

Anyway, we're going to have the bridal shower right here in the garden. I have a month and a half to get it looking its best. Right now it looks okay in different areas but not as a whole. Only the nasturtium stands out in the backyard. I planted the seeds two months ago and it's blasting with vibrant orange flowers. Some people consider nasturtium a weed, but, hey, anything that blooms so easily is just fine with me. The yellow dahlia is doing really well too and the princess flower next to it is about to bloom.

Another plant that's been flourishing is the star cluster. It's been blooming all summer with ruby red little flowers and hasn't needed much attention. The purple and red penstemons next to it are going wild too. They came back from last year, bigger and bushier than ever, and they've made us proud. The garden is actually looking pretty good right now, but it's a never-ending work of art, and I always feel that it still needs something.

July

July

JULY 1

We've been out bashing agapanthus. All over the roads, agapanthus. We just don't get it. What's so great about this plant?
It has a plethora of long leaves and a couple of small, faded blue,
flyaway flowers. We were driving home from the beach going on
about this. Then we turned back to the daylily and got all over
its case. It is said to be an incredible plant—disease resistant and
prolific. But, to us, it's a bust so far. Bill was going on about the
daylily not being so great, until I read him an article stating that
it had won the Award of Merit from the British Royal Horticul-
tural Society. He said, "Oh, what do they know?"

We stopped at Petaluma Garden Growers, one of my favorite
nurseries, on the way home. We walked every aisle and then ar-
gued about what we should get. We promised to limit ourselves
to two plants each. We wanted to try new things, so we got a
Russian sage, an unusual hibiscus, a new red yarrow, and a deep
purple delphinium. We arrived home at dusk, peeked out of the
car window to make sure the neighbors weren't watching, then
sneaked the plants into the backyard. We waited until we knew
everyone was inside eating supper, then we put on our gardening clothes and went digging. We got very involved in the garden work and decided it still looked bad, so we went around
pruning everything that didn't look healthy. We went wild on the
African daisy in front of the fence; it was getting brown and dry
and tangled. Now it looks neat. That's another great plant. It's a
prolific drought-tolerant groundcover. We don't water it and we
hardly look at it, yet it comes up blooming each spring.

After almost three hours of yardwork, we showered and then
had dinner, a perfect recipe from Martha Stewart's *Living* magazine, of course. I made an incredible spicy basil-cilantro dipping

sauce for grilled prawns. It was delicious! I Xeroxed the recipe for my sisters. I'd send them the magazine, but they'd have trouble believing Martha was for real.

JULY 2

At 6:00 A.M. the first ripe Santa Rosa plum fell from the tree. We were packing our bikes and climbing gear in the car to get away for the Fourth of July weekend. We sat down and ate the plum and a bunch of brand new strawberries. Bill was rambling on about climbing such and such mountains and I was quietly freaking out internally. I was scared to climb. Plus, last night's dreams were filled with old memories, and I woke up tired of myself. I dreamed about the bicentennial Independence Day almost twenty years ago. My sisters and I were visiting Daddy in Washington, D.C., where he was on assignment for the summer. We were on the lawn of the Capitol watching the fireworks. It was a spectacular show, but I sat there crying quietly to myself, thinking the whole time about my mother, who was sitting home alone in New York without a celebration. I had talked to her that morning on the phone and she had been crying. I wanted to fix everything and make it better; I still do. As much as I try to make a clean slate in my mind, these memories still haunt me.

By this point Bill had gotten into his old climbing stories of the Tetons, the Garden of the Gods, and Estes Park. He finally said, "Babe, are you listening to me?" I said, "No." So he started all over again. He loves telling these old climbing stories. Max pounced on top of Maui and that stopped the storytelling session, thank God. Bill was off chasing them. I went around the yard and power-watered all the plants. We'll be gone for three days, so I gave a ton of water to the plants that are not on the timer system. I might've drowned them. Max followed me around the vegetable garden stopping at each plant to admire the new growth. I'd say within a week or so we'll have ripe tomatoes, peppers, and cucumbers. I don't know what Max wanted. He must've sensed that we were leaving and he probably wondered who will be feeding him. You never know with cats. They're always trying to fake you out. Last time we went away, he got trapped in the shed and was locked in solitary confinement for two days. Bill keeps telling me it was an accident.

At 7:00 A.M., we took our coffees and hit the road. We drove for three hours listening to Van Morrison, then my favorite radio program, *Car Talk,* came on. I think I love the *Car Talk* brothers because they remind me of my relatives. I'm not sure if that's good or bad.

By 11:00 we were almost out of civilization. We pulled over to a pay phone in the middle of nowhere so I could call Ma to tell her that I wouldn't be calling her.

JULY 3

Today I hate Bill's guts. What made me think I wanted to marry him? Was I out of my mind? I'm so angry I could kill him, but I'm stranded here in the middle of the boonies trying to find my way to Pucci's cabin. I just walked away from Bill in a big huff. I don't care if he thinks I'm a bitch because I know that I'm not. It all began early this morning. I told Bill I wanted to be alone with him for my first real rock climb. I didn't want to have Mr. Louie and Pucci's perfect, super athletic, no-fear-in-them twenty-year-old sons, watching me try to get up a rock. He finally agreed and the boys went off hiking without us.

Bill and I took our harnesses, a rope, climbing shoes, and sandwiches and headed out into the Northern Sierras. It was a two-hour-long hike and I was bored. I don't see what's so great about hiking. I still think there are mass murderers waiting out there and that all the trees look the same. Anyway, we got to the rocks and Bill gave me a detailed lesson on all the climbing terminology. I wasn't afraid yet. I was still naive and curious. I watched him in awe as he climbed up the rock and hooked up the rope to the boulder above it. Then he rappeled down so gracefully it was like watching a dancer. I was still calm and I was impressed with his style. He could've done it with his eyes closed. It was just like when we're out cycling on gigantic hills and he speeds downhill with his arms stretched out, while I'm pressing on my brakes so hard every second that my fingers hurt at the end of the ride. He's disgusting. He came over to me with the harness and the rope and helped me to put it on and watched me do the figure-eight knot that he had taught me. The second I was all tightened up and ready to take the first step . . . I lost it. I started shaking and I broke into a cold sweat and had to go to the bathroom really bad. I ripped the whole harness off me like a madwoman and ran off into the bushes. When I returned I was still shaking. Bill was patient and tried to give me a pep talk, but I couldn't hear it. All I kept thinking was how much I hated him, because this was so easy for him and so fucking hard for me.

I ranted and raved for a while, on and on about how much I hated all the stupid trees and all the dumb rocks and the lakes and the whole wilderness in general. Why would anyone want to climb a mountain anyway? Like that's normal? So I walked away pissed off at the world and blamed Bill. He collected all the climbing gear and we walked for two hours in silence back to the cabin.

JULY 4

Today I am *sooo* in love with Bill! I woke him up this morning with the Hydroblaster, as payback for watching me suffer yesterday. At sunset last night, Pucci forced us together to talk. We drank merlot on the cabin porch overlooking the lake, while the boys, Surrey, Devon, and Rhodes, blasted Jane's Addiction annoyingly in the background. They actually call that music! Bill and I talked about expectations, character, strength, patience, and trust. That about covered it all, and I'd say we can get married now. I looked over the lake and at the family of geese sailing by and said I was sorry to the wilderness for bashing it yesterday. Not all trees look alike (just some). I crave to be part of it and beg to be accepted in Mother Nature's miraculous club.

This is July 4, Independence Day and Grandpa's birthday! Well into his seventies he used to sing "Happy Birthday you you." I guess the Yiddish-English translation threw him off somewhere.

It's an Independence Day I won't soon forget. It was a great day, and the sisterhood stands proud! We headed out early this morning on our mountain expedition to climb at Lover's Leap— Mr. Louie; Pucci; her no-fear, perfect, twenty-year-old, athletic sons; our recently divorced and cynical dear friend, Ron; Bill; and myself. We were all carrying tons of climbing gear, water, and food. (Somehow I ended up carrying the chocolate and the Coffee Nips. Do I rule, or what?) There was absolutely no way I was going to climb in front of those kids, who didn't have one iota of body fat, but I brought my climbing shoes anyway. I checked out the trees and Pucci pointed out the differences to me. She can't believe that I think they look alike; I can't believe she can't believe me.

We walked near Ron so that we could comfort him about his divorce that's been dragging on for the last three years. It's so hard to watch two people who really love each other break up because they fight all the time—I mean constantly, for years. Not just a few stupid fights about money or the dishes, but all the time. So they're slowly trying to go their own separate ways. I swear the day that I marry Bill we'll be together until the end. I simply don't have the stomach for divorce; it's too raw for me. It may seem naive, but I really do believe that our love will last, because we won't jeopardize it. It's too delicate and too precious to tamper with. Once you start rocking the boat, it takes work to get it back on course. We've been there; we've been on each other's very last nerve, and I can happily say, so far, we've made it back alive.

I caught up to Bill, and he was telling the boys the story about climbing in Rocky Mountain National Park twenty years ago during a three-day snowstorm. Bill and Mr. Louie had been freezing as they tried to climb a series of peaks along the Continental Divide before dark. They had gone as far as possible, so they set up camp for the night, camp being a windswept ridge at ten thousand feet. They didn't have a a tent, only two sleeping bags and a tiny useless tarp that the wind blew over regularly throughout the night as the storm raged on. They barely slept. When Bill woke up at 5:30 A.M., the storm was getting worse and Mr. Louie was sitting up, frozen, eating a Tiger's Milk bar. The only words he said were "We gotta get high and stay low."

Bill claims those were Mr. Louie's only true words of wisdom, ever.

Well, the hike was all fine and dandy until we got to the cliffs. I looked up and immediately felt severe butterflies in my stomach. Mr. Louie led the pitch. He went straight up the rock with rope and some beaners as if there was nothing to it. Does anything scare these guys? I mean it's not normal to scale the face of a rock . . . is it? What is their problem?

Pucci and I sat there for two hours reading our books and watching the boys take turns climbing. I was reading *The Dharma Bums* and had just read about Jack Kerouac struggling his way up the Matterhorn. He was afraid, and I loved him for admitting that he was scared to death.

I wanted to climb, I really did. I guess Bill knew that, because he came over to me and told me I could do it. Since I was so in love with him today, I believed him. So I put on my harness and tied myself into the rope. Mr. Louie was above and Ron and Bill were next to me on the ground giving me moral support. I made it halfway up the face of the rock and then I got exhausted. Then it happened. Since the rope was at an angle for the guys who were doing the more advanced climbs, when my feet let go of the wall, instead of just hanging there, I quickly swung about thirty feet across the rock, hit my head and shoulder, spun out of control, and was finally lowered to the ground in shock. I tried to hold back my tears, but they started flowing, and I started screaming at all those confident fools for lying to me about how "easy" rock climbing is and how anyone can do it. I stood there for five minutes cursing them out and this whole rock climbing thing. I told them they should get a life! I was incredibly angry and totally out of control.

A few minutes later, Bill came over looking very concerned. He said they were packing up and getting ready to go home. I don't know what came over me at that moment, but I told them to stop, that I wanted to climb. I had them set up a safer belay so that the rope was not at an angle. They all worked quietly getting it set. No one spoke. I think they were afraid of me. I was sweaty and shaky on the outside, but on the inside I knew that I would make it to the top. Something strong and intangible inside of me was pushing me. I struggled up, pissed off at the world, tired of being afraid. I was fed up with it and I wanted to prove to myself and to all the testosterone below me that I could do it. After all the feminist propaganda I've forced into these boys over the years, I knew I simply had no choice.

After each step I took I would turn around and look down to see how far up I was and would see Ron's and Bill's little faces smiling up at me. When I was about three quarters of the way up, there was an overhang. This was the most challenging part of the climb and I used every inch of strength in my arms and legs to carry me over it. When I arrived on the upper part of it, I looked up and I could finally see Mr. Louie's smirking face towering over me. When I made it up to the top, I hugged and kissed Mr. Louie. It was the first time in seven years that we were genuinely kind to each other. I could tell he was getting that awkward don't-crowd-me guy thing, so I walked away and sat by myself.

I looked over the beautiful valley down below and I was hypnotized by it. I fell in love with it. A year ago I would have never done this. Maybe people can change, if they really want to. Maybe there's a power deep inside all of us waiting to be found.

A power that gives us strength and makes us believe that any-thing is possible.

I felt like I was in heaven.

JULY 6

When we arrived home Monday night, the garden was strug-gling. There had been a heat wave while we were away and many of the plants looked dried out and close to death. As Bill unpacked the car, I ran around with the hose feverishly soaking every-thing. I guess drowning them three days ago didn't do the trick. I was most concerned about the rudbeckia, which looked dan-gerously droopy. But by morning, everything was perky and alive! It's amazing how flowers bounce back to life from a little water.

I didn't have to work, so I spent the day pampering the yard, and in between pulling weeds, I called my sisters and all my girl-friends to brag about my mountain-climbing fall. I wanted to call Ma, but I couldn't tell my mother that I had swung off a cliff. She'd come up here and hit Bill with her pocketbook and yell at him for taking me into the woods, "where there were no normal people." But I did go on in great detail with Sha and Ca. My sis-ters and I have a tendency to exaggerate, and by the time Bill came home from work, he said the story had become so embel-lished that it sounded something like this: There we were in the middle of an avalanche in Northern Africa and there I was, an American woman, alone, swinging one hundred feet across the north face of Kilimanjaro to save mankind.

I took Bill on a nature walk at sunset. A few weeks ago we had planted something new and exciting. It's called ipomoea, or blue dawn flower, and looks like morning glory. It's an extremely fast-growing vine with big, bright blue flowers that fade into pink. It's one of my latest favorites and scores an A+ on my re-port card.

Then I dragged Bill over to my rose garden and showed him

the intense job of weeding out the bermuda grass I had accomplished today. The garden still looks a little crowded, so I decided I would give my Graham Thomas English rose to Eleanor, the eighty-year-old biddy with the hollyhocks, who lives down the road. She's out there watering her garden every day by hand. I guess she doesn't know that soaker hoses have been invented. She comes alive whenever she talks about her flowers, especially her dahlias. In some ways she's my idol. When I'm an old biddy, I want to be just like Eleanor Dahaney, and I want to have hollyhocks like hers and a huge straw sun hat with old sunglasses from the fifties and a gardening apron with a big smiling sunflower on it.

JULY 8

This morning I was running late for work, but having been taught by my mother and being the compulsive that I am, I had to make the bed before leaving the house. Maui was asleep at the foot of the bed on top of Bill's purple sweatshirt. I shooed her off and began frantically fluffing the sheets. She jumped up on the dresser and watched me from above. Each tuck and each pillow fluff, she rolled her eyes and yawned as if I was taking too long. When the bed was finally beautifully made, she hopped down from her throne and curled herself perfectly in the middle of Bill's pillow and stared at me like I was bothering her. Her face told me that my work was done . . . adequately, and that I was now dismissed.

God, I want her life.

JULY 10

Today we drove down to Santa Cruz to meet with Charlie and work out the wedding ceremony. Charlie's garden is phenomenal, beautiful and perfect without being too perfect. It makes you want to tear your entire garden up and start over! He's worked it for close to ten years and it is truly an inspiration and a goal I can aspire to. I went around with my camera, taking pictures of all the plants I wanted to get or transplant in our yard to make it look like his. We decided that you're allowed to plagiarize in gardening. You can steal your friend's ideas and put them in your own garden. It's kind of a compliment to the original gardener. I would be honored if anyone wanted to learn from our garden, but it's still too dull to have a following.

Charlie has an intricate brick layout throughout the perennial garden. Tomorrow I'm off to buy more bricks for my rose garden. That's exactly what it needs to help smother the bermuda grass. I'm so excited. I probably won't sleep tonight because I'll be designing the bricks in my head. This is when Bill calls me a nerd. But I happen to know that when he was doing the brick-work around the vegetable garden, he woke up at three o'clock one morning and worked until sunrise just because he was so involved in the project — so he's a dweeb too. He just won't admit that he's obsessed; he's obviously got real deep-rooted problems that he's not in touch with.

Charlie, his partner Tracey, Bill, and I sat in their perfect backyard and had toast with homemade raspberry jam. Charlie updated us on Ron's painful and expensive divorce. They've all been friends since college days and have witnessed Ron's relationship from beginning to end. As I listen to stuff about all these divorces, I wonder why anyone bothers to get married anymore. But I guess you just have to say to yourself that you're willing to take on the challenge, climb the mountain and see what happens. I think we're brought up to believe that we will marry one day and live happily ever after. No one tells you how much work it is to keep a relationship alive. Everyone just expects bliss and happiness from the wedding day on. I mean, marriage ain't no picnic and it's not about me, me, me. We are put on this earth to help each other. There is crime and disease and poverty waiting for us all just around the corner and if we are lucky enough in this life to have true love, a couple of good friends and family, our health, a job, and a nice cup of coffee from time to time, then we should consider ourselves blessed.

Today I feel a little sad, sad for all those love affairs and marriages that didn't work out. Sad for all those people who said they loved each other and then when they felt betrayed and grew bitter, hired a lawyer and took the skin off the other's back to let them know just how much they "loved" them.

JULY 11

This morning Charlie, Bill, and I walked to the beach and I watched Charlie and Bill swim. They're both close to forty years old but they still have young, healthy, gorgeous bodies. They looked like little kids, they were having so much fun swimming and splashing around in the water. I sat on a blanket and enjoyed the hot sun on my face.

When the guys were done swimming, we began writing the ceremony—a mixture of Judaism, Christianity, Buddhism, and American Indian. (My mother will just flip.) Charlie will read the ceremony, and then we agreed to write our own personal vows to each other. I can't wait to write them. I have so much to say to Bill, but he just rolled his eyes. I know him well enough to know that he'll probably write a set of rocket scientist vows at the last minute, and they will be the size of a book and brilliant.

JULY 12

Today was a pruning kind of day. I trimmed all the overgrown hedges in the front yard and then attacked the spent flowers on the perennials. After that I painted the exterior window trims with a blue paint like I'd been wanting to do for a few weeks now. While waiting for the paint to dry, I transplanted a few plants. The weather has finally cooled off enough to put some new plants in the ground. The yard is looking better, but there's still so much to be done. At sunset, when Bill pulled into the driveway, I had the maxipower hedge trimmer in one hand and the large pruning shears in the other. I was covered with mud, paint, and sweat from head to toe and looked posessed. Bill walked right by me and went straight into the house.

I'm not sure if he was pretending he didn't know me or if he was afraid of me.

JULY 14

Yesterday, during an interview for a short film project, an interesting thing happened. I was dressed very nicely in a white suit and I exuded competence and power. I was doing great; sounding intelligent, getting all the colloquialisms correct, nodding my head, agreeing, disagreeing, etc. Then I looked down at my hands and noticed that I still had soil and dirt in my fingernails from my little spurt of last-minute gardening that morning. (If I have an extra minute or two in the morning, even while walking from the front door to the car, I'll find things to do in the garden — weeds to pull, flowers to stake up, roses to talk to.) From then on, I was so aware of my hands and trying to cover them up that I don't remember what the hell I was talking about and I just wanted the interviewer to shut up so I could go home and scrub my hands. When we said goodbye I shook his hand tightly with both of mine to cover up any dirty fingernails. Now he probably thinks I'm too caring a person to be in the film business and I'll never get the job!

JULY 24

Well, I got the job and it sucks! It's finally the weekend. I worked with an old has-been TV actress this week. She was nasty and complained all day long about her trailer, her car phone, her hair person, her suite, and the schedule. Later I found out that she was making half a million dollars for these two weeks of work. I mean, it's not like we're curing cancer. She doesn't even have a clue.

Today, after the crew sat around for an hour waiting for her, she refused to come out of her trailer. Jim, the director and I went over to her motorhome. She talked his ear off about the ridiculous schedule, the hours, and how tired she was. (She did have a point. TV movie schedules are getting tighter and tighter and each department is given less crew members and expected to do more work, faster and for less money. This way the above the line gang can make bigger salaries, buy expensive houses, and drive fancier cars.) After a few minutes of listening to her problems, I realized that I was being a phony by pretending to look like I cared, so I left. On the way out of her trailer, I took the untouched hundred-dollar fruit and nut platter, that the producer had given her five days ago. I walked down the street and gave it to the three homeless guys sitting on the corner. Some of the motorhome drivers witnessed this and as I passed them they said "God bless you, Annie." I figured that it was a positive omen to be blessed by the teamsters. They certainly must be very tight with God, or how else would they be making so much money watching the rest of us work, while they sit around eating donuts and reading the newspaper?

JULY 26

This morning we went out and ate the first fig on the fig tree. The fig tree was a gift from my mother when we first moved in here. Figs are great trees because they're easy, they grow fast, and they produce a lot of fruit. The figs are sweet and taste like candy. We also brought in our first six red Early Girl tomatoes, for salad tonight. When we came back inside, Ma called. She said, "Hi Mouse, I'm watching your friend, Martha Stewart. She's talking about sunflowers."

I said, "Ma, she's not my friend."

She said, "What do you mean she's not your friend? She should be honored to be your friend!"

JULY 28

I know that I'm obsessed and should possibly be considered dangerous in a nursery, but the only thing that makes me feel better about myself is the fact that Bill has become obsessed with composting. Last week he had our friend Mooney build him an extravagant, expensive, redwood compost bin. I had been on location all week and came home Friday night at 10:30. I took a shower and put on my Victoria's Secret silk shorts wedding outfit from Ca and poured two glasses of merlot. I was just about to kiss Bill in the kitchen when he dragged me out into the backyard with my eyes closed. By flashlight, he showed me the new compost land and explained the whole procedure—which part is for food, which part is for old dead plants that get the boot, how to stir and mix the bins, and the finished product: beautiful, nutritious, black soil. He was so proud of his composter.

Then we sat on the red bench, in the dark, and he told me about the ranch up the road that gave him free horse manure for the compost bin. I stopped him midsentence and asked him if he had noticed that I wasn't wearing my flannel pajamas, but lingerie. He said: "Yeah, babe, that's great. You look nice," and went on about how to age horse shit.

I was too tired to kill him.

JULY 29

First thing this morning, I woke up with a burning desire to make a fresh bouquet of flowers for the table. I went around the yard picking liatris, rudbeckia, dahlia, Peruvian lilies, roses, and small gladiolas. It felt so good to be home and not to have a million plans for the day. The flower arrangement looked beautiful, and I felt good about myself.

Cat and Randy stopped by to drop off a book for Bill, and poor Randy was whisked off into the backyard for a compost show-and-tell. I have a feeling that no one is safe anymore. Anyone who dares to come over to our house will have to get the grand tour of our garbage mixed with some old leaves, dead flowers, insects, and horse shit.

I hope they, too, find it simply fascinating.

JULY 30

Twenty luscious, red tomatoes off the vine. This is astonishing. I put all the tomatoes, peppers, eggplants, and cucumbers on the red bench and took close-up pictures to send to Ma. Right above them the morning glory and the passion flower are blooming away and it looks gorgeous.

This morning I saw Liisa again. I've grown to love her because she taught me to be silent and hear the voice of the soul. I told her about my phone call with Celina, Daddy's second wife. She had called me this week and asked if I would be more comfortable if she didn't come out for the wedding. I was painfully honest and told her that it would be such a relief for me not to have to be stressed out about having her and my mother in the same room. I said that she was very much invited but that if she didn't make it, everybody would understand. I know that wasn't the most grown-up answer and that I'm still protecting my mother, but it was the truth. I wanted us all to have fun and not add more pressure to an already boiling situation. In the long run, Celina should be relieved too. She probably realized the harsh territory she'd be entering, surrounded by all of our boisterous relatives. Between Ma and Uncle Bob, there's always the distinct possibility of being zapped with a zinger that could very easily destroy your day and possibly your entire life.

When I returned home, Sha called. She was in a huff because

she had just talked to Ma and they had an argument about the weather. I can just imagine the scintillating conversation! If anyone heard some of the phone calls with my mother and the four of us, they would wonder why we'd ever bother to call her again. Our friends would run away from us, realizing that we were sick, weak, codependent lunatics! They don't know the good side of her, the side that came to all of our Brownie and PTA meetings, the side that took the bus uptown in a blizzard to my band recital to hear my bassoon solo, the side that was always the life of the party, the side that loved to watch us eat, the side that told us we could do anything. The one that told us to speak up to social injustice, the one that told us we were beautiful, the one that put a note in our lunch bags every day, the one that took us skating in Central Park, the one that told us to live life fully, appreciate what we had, and be kind to everyone no matter what color or class, the one that tucked us in bed every night and told us that there was a silver lining around every cloud.

After my phone call with Sha, I paced around the garden, trying once again to make sense of all this. For years I tried to change my mother. It was my goal. I wanted to save her from her abusive childhood. But today I've finally accepted the fact that we can't change people. They have to change themselves and there are a lot of people who don't want to change—people who will never see the whole picture, especially your side. Blaming them won't get you far. I did it for years. It's like getting up every morning, hitting your head against the wall twenty times, and then going out into the world and trying to have a nice day. Once you're done being angry all you can do is love them. Even if it means keeping some distance and learning to say no, so that you can take care of yourself. Maybe by healing ourselves, we can break the cycle, and possibly mend the broken spirits of past generations.

August

August

AUGUST 1

The big *W* is less than a month away. This morning, while I was burning the raisin toast (like I do almost every morning), Bill came into the kitchen in deep thought. He said that he had figured me out. He told me that I underestimate myself 75 percent of the time and overestimate myself 25 percent of the time.

Then he went out and fed the cats.

AUGUST 5

It was an incredible weekend. I had a bridal-barbeque-shower that wasn't too "girlie." Ca came up for the weekend, and the hollyhocks and the sunflowers in the front yard bloomed. Can't ask for more than that, can you?

I usually detest Bridal showers, but today I had a great time. Ca, Cat, Gwyneth, Cecily, Sandy, Elissa, Pucci, and Ellen were all together in my backyard. I wore my new yellow flowery dress, but that's as girlie as it got. No foolish games were allowed, because that stuff gets on my nerves. No gifts were allowed (except some snuck in). There's a lot of greed surrounding this wedding thing. All these gifts and outfits that your poor friends have to buy, and most of my friends don't have a lot of money. I know cutesy bridal shower gifts are supposed to be fun, but to me it's just irritating and I'm too old for that. When I get a bunch of brilliant women together I'd rather be productive than ooh and aah at silly little things. A group of smart and uppity women is too powerful a commodity to waste on trivial stuff.

I decided to have party favors. They consisted of applications to the Working Assets long-distance phone company and credit

card (where 1 percent of your bill goes to fifty charitable organizations) as well as registration forms to vote and information
on Emily's List, the organization that promotes women political
candidates who will support bills that protect women and im-
prove the quality of their lives. When we support so-called
women's issues (which really should be called people issues),
such as bills on child care, child support, pay equity, sexual harassment, domestic violence, family leave, and healthcare, we are
actually improving the quality of an entire family's life. Right here
at my wedding-a-go-go shower! We owe it to the next generation not to sit around like couch potatoes, complaining, but to
know the issues and get involved.

Once we solved the world's problems, we grilled some delicious chicken. Gwyneth made a peanut sauce that was out of this
world. We were practically drinking it. We also had homegrown
lettuce, tomatoes, cucumbers, and peppers. We drank wine and
discussed philosophy, gardening, work, cinema, politics, food, lipstick, and men. Elissa gave me the book *Backlash: The Undeclared
War Against American Women.* I'm sure I'll love it, but I don't think
it's the right book to read during our honeymoon.

Then everyone started asking me questions about the wedding
and that made me nervous. They asked about a seating plan,
name tags, the receiving line, and things I had never even thought
about or heard of. I realized I should have read that bridal etiquette book instead of ripping it apart! I explained to them that
all I know is there is the A, B, and C list. All of them were on the
A list, luckily. The C list consists of people we're obligated to invite. I shouldn't have mentioned it, because they all started going
off about being privileged to be on the A list.

I can tell I'll never hear the end of this.

Then we had Gwyneth's and Elissa's sons, Miles and David,
break the piñata. It was the only semi-game allowed, and it
was mainly for the kids. All sorts of colorful candy and sex
toys fell out. (I know this must've been Cat's idea.) The kids
went around picking up the big, plastic cucumber, the nude
male and female toothbrushes, and some fruit-flavored rubbers;

nothing fazed them. They dropped all the sex toys back on the floor, scooped up the lollipops and chocolate, and walked away pleased.

AUGUST 6

Today Ca and I drove out to Point Reyes to hike Mt. Wittenberg. At first we thought we'd never make it out of the parking lot. We walked about two hundred yards in the hot, blistering sun, stopped, looked at each other, and fell down laughing. We were both thinking the same thing. Should we just forget about the hike and go shopping? But we got hold of ourselves and faced the mountain. We talked about how it would be seeing Uncle Bob, Aunt Ceil, and Cousin Sue at the wedding. We felt bad about the scene we made seven years ago when Cousin Sue gave birth to Katie and we went to visit them in the hospital. It was nighttime. Katie was premature, so we watched her through a glass window. Sue and John were in the room with her — dreamy-eyed new parents. It was a beautiful, tender moment, but Ca had to blow it and get us thrown out of the hospital by the head nurse. We just couldn't handle the fact that Cousin Sue had grown up and wasn't our perfect, bossy teenage cousin anymore, the one who made us organize our closet each time she'd visit and then would score big points with Ma. Ca said something about the paper dolls we played with at Aunt Ceil's house, and for some reason that had us tearing down the intensive care corridor in hysterics. We were holding our stomachs, laughing so hard that we were crying. Then the big, fat head nurse, who had just chased Uncle Bob out of the nurses' station, came over and lifted us by our collars and dumped us on the sidewalk, where we continued to roll on the ground for another ten minutes laughing.

I don't know what it is, but I've never laughed so hard with anyone else. Ca just has to look at me at the right moment and it's all over. After our four-hour hike, during which I recited all the names of the wildflowers just to get on her nerves, we headed for the mall to find wedding shoes. I'm telling you, the hardest thing about the wedding outfit is finding the right shoes! They're all so geeky.

Well, we shopped till we dropped. Literally. We ended up delirious, on a dressing room floor, laughing because Ca was about to miss her flight because of a sale! The saleswoman must have thought that we were drunk. Our eyes were all red and watery. We crawled out of the dressing room to the cash register, and Ca, in her serious doctor tone, asked the counter girl to please hurry up because she had a flight to catch.

The peppy and much too happy counter girl said, "You betcha!"

That sent us right over the edge . . . again.

AUGUST 7

Cat gave me something very special today. It was an excerpt from a 1950 high school home economics textbook called "How to Be a Good Wife."

Have dinner ready. Plan ahead to have a delicious meal on time. This is a good way to let him know that you have been thinking about him and are concerned with his needs. Most men are hungry when they come home. Touch up your makeup, put a ribbon in your hair, and look fresh. At the time of his arrival, eliminate all noise of the washer, dryer, dishwasher, or vacuum. Prepare the children. They are little treasures, and he would like to see them playing the part. Listen to him. You may have a dozen things to tell him, but the moment of his arrival is not the time. Let him talk first. Have a cool or warm drink ready for him. Arrange his pillow and offer to take off his shoes. Speak in a low, soft, soothing pleasant voice. Be gay and a little more interesting.

No wonder our mothers are all messed up.

AUGUST 8

Eve called today. She will be in Europe during the wedding so she won't be able to make it. She was such an integral part of my single life in New York. She was my escape from the film industry, from all the wrong men, and from lonely Saturday nights. For years she sublet a wonderful loft from a famous artist. It had beautiful blond wood floors and walls and skylights in every room. The bathrooms had double shower heads so you could shower next to your friend and not hog all the water. What a concept! We went through a macrobiotic stage, but it didn't last long. We made all sorts of healthy dishes in this loft and listened to jazz on sunny Sunday mornings. I always have fond memories of a relaxing getaway in the heart of New York City. Eve was in graduate school studying psychology and now she's a real live doctor. Most of my work friends never met her since she was my sanctuary away from the chaotic film life. Now she won't be coming to the wedding and no one will believe that she ever really existed.

However, all of Bill's close friends from chiropractic school will be attending — people like Charlie, Ron, Brent, Alex, Wendy, Patti, and Barbara, who were in the same class as Ca and Bill. Barbara is the only person I know who even comes close to competing with Ca for power talking. Supposedly they were in trouble all the time in the back row of class because they couldn't keep their mouths shut.

Julie, her sister Donna, and baby Jack will be coming out from the East Coast. Years ago, when we were wild and crazy production assistants in New York City, Donna and I sneaked into a Tina Turner concert at Madison Square Garden. We were filming a movie across the street with John Lithgow (an honorary member of the sisterhood because he's such a good guy. That night Donna and I took our walkie-talkies, put gaffer's tape on them, and wrote "Stage Crew" on the tape. I walked about fifty feet in front of her, passing forty security guards and police, through massive hallways and elevators, speaking "tech talk" on our walkies until we were both safely down in the eleventh row. Tina would've been proud! "What's Love Got to Do With It" had just come out and she was hot.

The next day we were the talk of the set!

Her sister, Julie and I became friends instantly. We were part of a big clique of New York production assistants that worked on all the movies in town. The only thing that got us through the stress, the low pay, and horrendous hours were the friendships we made along the way. There were many days the Director would be screaming at us to lock up a busy Manhattan intersection and the ten p.a.'s would work with the New York police department to close down the street. After a while, especially if I was working with my good friends Julie, Sardi, Parnes, Don, Steve, Tony A., Greenhut, and Vince, we would stand a block away from camera, out of earshot, pointing and waving our arms as if we were seriously setting up a major lockup. But what we really were talking about was what a shithead the First A.D. was, where we were going out partying Friday night, and who on the crew we thought was cute. Those were the good old days.

AUGUST 10

At seven o'clock this morning, I waved goodbye to Bill. He's off to the mountains for his bachelor party. Mr. Louie organized a rock climbing trip with Bill's friends Ron, Randy, Rick, a couple of Pucci's fearless sons. When we were packing last night, I had this premonition that I would never see him again and that I wouldn't have to go to the wedding. The closer it gets to the day, the more dismal thoughts I have about something happening to me or him. I hope this is normal. It was hard saying goodbye to him this morning. Usually it's me that's running off to go on location, blowing him kisses. I like it better that way; I don't like to be the one that's left behind.

I went to a gardening class at Green Gulch Farm. The

fields of flowers and vegetables are breathtaking. We made dry flower arrangements of roses, English lavender, yarrow, and strawflower. You cut them with a long stem and then hang them upside down in a dark, dry, airy place. They came out great. Yo, eat your heart out, Martha! On the way home, I was thinking of Bill as I sang along with Van Morrison, "I want you to be my ball and chain." I was having a grand old time until I got stuck in traffic behind an old exhaust-belching truck. Not only was this truck polluting the entire freeway but it had wheel mud flaps with that nude babe on them. I thought those went out in the sixties! I finally passed it, took my sunglasses off, and glared at the driver. He was smoking a cigarette, of course, and looked at me, grinning. He thought I was flirting with him! That's just so typical.

I stopped at a newsstand to get the paper, and the day proceeded to get worse. I opened up the pink section, and the three movies that were playing next to our house were starring Vandamme, Schwarzenegger, and Bruce Willis. Like I'm going to pay a dime to see those three testoterone-filled, violence-promoting, jerks. The next step down in the vicious cycle of profit-making producers, is the ignorant consumer who supports such depthless and repugnant filmmaking with no social value. And if I hear the line "I only went to see it for the special effects," one more time, I'll scream! What a bunch of crap.

I decided the real world was too much with me and went home to hide in my garden. I finished the book *Angle of Repose* by Wallace Stegner. A true masterpiece. Part of the story chronicles a three-generations-old family rose garden. An author after my own heart! It's been Bill's favorite book for years, and he gave it to me last week as a prewedding gift. Now I can marry him. Anyone who loves Wallace Stegner is way up there on my list.

In the evening I went around and fed all the roses with fish emulsion dissolved in two gallons of water. The most outstanding performers of this summer have been Bonica, Golden Showers, Iceberg, Cecile Brunner, and Ballerina. Since May, I've been feeding all of the roses with a balanced fertilizer during the first week of the month and with Epsom salt during the third week of the month. I stopped feeding them epsom salt at the beginning of July. I try to follow the rose diet Rayford uses at Garden Valley Ranch Nursery in Petaluma, because Rayford is my hero.

AUGUST 12

Since Bill wasn't around today, I was bad, bad, bad. I drove out to Sloat Garden Center, where they were having a 30-percent-off-perennials sale! I was there at nine o'clock sharp, waiting outside the gate like a true geek. I walked down every aisle, hypnotized. I didn't go too crazy because I wasn't about to spend the entire day planting stuff. I bought a blue clematis for the back fence, a dark red dahlia to go near the angelic yellow dahlia, three rare salvias, and some impatiens for the shade area in the front. When I got up to the checkout counter, I started chatting away with the owner. Gardeners are really a bunch of nerds and love to share plant stories. In any other kind of store, I quietly do my business and don't talk to anyone, but at the nursery I ask a million questions and even give my little bit of advice to the new gardeners wandering around lost. They're easy to spot. They stutter when they try to pronounce bougainvillea or hydrangea or rhododendron.

Anyway, I was rambling on with the owner about all my relatives coming out next week to visit and how I wanted the garden to look great. You see, I'm always going on and on about my garden on long-distance phone calls with them. All my friends and family must think they're going to encounter Monet's garden! Parts of our garden are beautiful and other parts are still a work in major progress. I told the owner that I was getting married next week and I wanted it to look spectacular for my wedding. I said it! I said it and I didn't even know that I was saying it! I remained calm and continued the conversation as if I was perfectly in control. As I was leaving the nursery, she waved goodbye and said, "Have a good one!"

Bill got home tonight from his swinging bachelor party in the mountains. He said he had a great time, but there were no babes in bikinis helicoptered in as Mr. Louie had promised. In fact, he said the highlight of the trip was when Rick accidentally hit himself, where it really hurts, with a bungee cord. They named the sacred waters there Bungee Ball Lake.

AUGUST 14

Last night, at ten o'clock, Bill dragged me outside and we climbed up the lawn furniture to the roof. We stayed up there for an hour or so waiting for the meteor. We waited and waited and waited but didn't see anything.

Figures.

While we waited for the meteor that never came, we planned our Alaska honeymoon, and Bill just had to bring up some of the old trips, like Maui. He can't seem to forget that trip, can he? We were camping in Haleakala Crater so that we could see the world renowned sunrise from there. I woke him up at 4:00 A.M., because my head was cold, and just before the brilliant sunrise hit, I got an eye infection and we had to drive down the mountain to the emergency room. When we returned the next day, it was foggy, and all day long we kept hearing people talking about how yesterday's magnificent sunrise was the only clear morning in weeks. If one more tourist talked about yesterday's stupid sunrise, I was going to smack him with my underwater camera. Then that evening there was a spectacular sunset and when Bill went to get his camera out of the rental car he found that I had locked the keys in it.

I keep telling him I'm usually not like that on vacation.

He doesn't believe me.

AUGUST 19

Okay, the reality has finally set in. Dad just called. He's at the airport renting a car and heading up here to start moving things along. He sounded so happy and eager that it woke me right up. Today is Monday. The wedding is Saturday. I haven't slept well. Last night I dreamed that I promised fidelity and regretted it in the morning.

AUGUST 22

Tuesday was a great day. First of all, Sha and Ca both called and sounded very excited. Then, to top it off, Ro flew in and we met for coffee. We haven't seen each other for about five years. It was awkward for a minute or two and then it was just like the old days. She looks beautiful as usual, especially for a woman with two twenty-year-old daughters. We talked about every-thing and everyone. We laughed and cried. Some things never change.

Wednesday it got even better. Barbara arrived from Colorado. She came along with Dad and me to Trader Joes. We bought six bottles of wine so that we could choose which kind of wine we wanted the restaurant to serve at the wedding. We went to a Thai restaurant and opened the three bottles of red and three bottles of white. We tasted each of them at eleven in the morning. We were having a blast. I haven't been so happy in years. We got home and we were all drunk. Dad went under his plum tree and took a nap while Barbara and I sat in the kitchen, under the warm sunny skylight, and drank apricot tea.

Today, Thursday, da-da-da-dum!, the Queen Bee arrived in the afternoon!

Did you feel the earth stop?

I went to her hotel room and she was the happiest I have ever seen her in my life. She was laughing and hugging and kissing. I felt so loved. She kissed my face all over like a puppy dog and I panted. I got all of her attention without having to share it with my sisters! We sat on her bed and she gave me her real pearl earrings that she had worn to her own wedding! Real jewelry. Wow! Just as we were falling in love with each other, there was a knock at the door. It was Ca and Ga. Ca hobbled in on her crutches and stole the whole show. Figures. She fell down her steps last week. (Yeah, right, like that wasn't planned. She probably threw herself down! One, two, three . . . *Go!*) Ga showed me her multicultural wedding outfit—something between a caftan and a sack of potatoes. Of course it sent Ca into hysterics on the bed. Then Ma started picking on Ga for making Ca get loud and wild. Then she said we were all getting on her nerves, kissed us all goodbye, and with a loud sigh of relief, threw us out of her hotel room.

Hel*lo?* Doesn't she know who I am? For crying out loud, I'm the bride!!! Sheesh!

We decided we'd go to my house. On the way out of the hotel, there was a big commotion in the lobby. Three young bellhops were unloading a car filled with boxes of champagne, party favors, cowboy hats, balloons, confetti, and plastic sunglasses. The front desk was crowded with guests checking in, but the clerks were busy Xeroxing and stapling wedding maps, schedules, group activities, and directions. I happened to look over and realized that they were directions to my wedding! In the middle of all this chaos was my "retired" father, supervising and delegating the entire front desk staff like a madman. He had those young little whippersnappers running around saying "Yes, sir." No sooner had we recognized Daddy than we noticed the reason there was such a long line at the front desk. Who else but Uncle Bob was there, with his white hair and his cane, trying to pick up the cute twenty-three-year-old assistant manager. His T-shirt said SURF'S UP and he smelled like vodka. I hadn't seen him in a few years. His health has been deteriorating, and I was flattered that he made it out to the West Coast at all. Every time I see him, I get tears in my eyes. He's one of those people, like Ma, who you love so much it hurts. Sometimes they bring you such happiness and other times they step on you so hard you break.

"What do you think? I'm some sort of dirty old man?" he said. He explained to us that he was trying to pick up Tanya, the assistant desk manager, for his son, cousin Peter, not for himself. He's been using that line for years. Aunt Ceil says if it keeps him out of her hair, it's a good thing. Dad proudly showed us the party hats and explained at great length how he was going to make our wedding a wild party, not a stiff formal fuddy-duddy event.

Since when did he get so cool?

AUGUST 23

A.M.   Twenty-four hours to go. I can't breathe. I seriously think I'm going to die.

Somebody help me.

Monogamy? *What was I thinking?*

P.M.   Ca, Ga, and I drove downtown early this morning to one of my favorite places on earth, the San Francisco Flower Market. Mr. Louie and Pucci met us there. A few months back, they offered to do the big flower arrangement for the ceremony. I don't know why I let Mr. Louie be in charge of this. This is the guy who accidentally taped over his own wedding videotape with a football game. But Pucci promised me that everything would be fine and I trust her. We had a couple hundred dollars to spend on FLOWERS!! Yay! I can be Martha Stewart today!!! Yiipppeee!!! It was like sending a kid into a candy store. At one point I was so overwhelmed that I was walking in circles staring at all the pretty flowers. Thank God Ga noticed. She took charge and forced me to make some decisions. Left alone, I would've still been wandering around there smelling the roses and would have missed my entire wedding.

For the altar, we bought twenty-five enormous, man-eating sunflowers mixed with some rare ivy and tall orange crocosmia. For the tables, we picked iris, tulips, liatris, delphinium, larkspur, and rudbeckia. Champagne roses were chosen for me and pink bouquets for the sisterhood. Getting the flowers was fun, but not as much fun as I thought it was going to be. It all became very exhausting and I just wanted to sleep for a few days. I had lost the ticket to get us out of the flower market parking lot and began arguing with the poor attendant. I was simply trying to reason with him that we had bought flowers and now were leaving, so it was maybe an hour or less that we were parked. He finally let us out of there without paying for the whole day. Ca got mad at me. She said I treated him like he was a poor parking p.a. and that I was bossing him around like I was on the set. In her little squeaky voice she said, "You people in the film business are rude and obnoxious and you make too much money and expect the whole world to be at your beck and call."

She was right.

I took her out to lunch and then she was nice to me again.

We spent the afternoon in the backyard arranging flowers. I was so impressed with Ca. She had her own little floral assembly line on the picnic table and she was working it! Then Cecily would take the completed vase and and tie ribbons around it. Pucci and I made bridal bouquets with the perfect little roses. Mr. Louie paced back and forth pondering how the hell he was going to make the sunflowers stand up straight at the altar. I'm glad that's not my duty. I'm starting to wonder. . . . I think he was torn between helping with the flowers or hanging out with the guys and drinking beer. So we put them all to work; no one was safe. Anyone who walked through that garden gate was given a flower assignment—there was no way around it. There they were, Bill's very best friends in the whole wide world, Ron, Rick, Charlie, Mr. Louie, and high school John, trying to arrange flowers while drinking beer and discussing baseball at the same time. And when Bill came home from work he had to join them. It was priceless. Then Ca came up with a great idea. She sent Bill and Ron off to the local pet shop to buy thirty goldfish to put in the round vases with the flowers tomorrow morning. I like that.

I wonder what Grandpa Max is thinking of all this as he

watches from above. Elissa's three-year-old son, David, asked if his deceased grandfather "was in a star." I hope tomorrow that Grandpa Max's star shines bright. He'll probably be up there shaking his head saying, "Oy, not another goy!"

At sunset we rehearsed the ceremony in the backyard. No one knew what they were doing, and everyone walked at the wrong time and at the wrong pace. Poor Charlie was trying to be serious, and we were all a mess. We finally made it through, and, just as we ended, we heard the Queen Bee's arrival. Da *da* da *dum!* Toot the trumpet! She came prancing into the backyard, passing a picnic table filled with empty beer glasses, and asked, "Hey, what's going on around here? Where's the party? Where's the bride?" We introduced her to Charlie, the minister. She said: "Oy, this is a minister? What is this? He's a kid. He looks like he's twelve! No, get somebody who knows what they're doing." Thank God Charlie knew how to deal with the Queen Bee. He instantly charmed his way into the Queen of Charm's heart by asking about her life story—how she fled from Persia, carrying her brothers, with no shoes, living on half a bagel. . . .

An hour later she told us, "This Charlie, he's a doll!"

At eight o'clock we went to meet the family for the prewedding dinner. Instead of it being a formal party, it was a bunch of loud New Yorkers eating at a Chinese restaurant in California. It was a blast! Everyone chattering excitedly, exotic and colorful dishes being passed around noisily, Dad and Uncle Bob, making a merry and witty toast, Sha and Jim's big arrival, Ga explaining multiculturalism to the Chinese waiter, who hardly spoke English, and me, sitting across from Bill, watching him while he kept two completely different conversations going as he sat in the hot seat, trapped alive between Ma and Uncle Bob.

MIDNIGHT   It's midnight. I can't sleep. When we got home from the restaurant, the house was so alive. All the guys were still awake and were sitting under the jessamine vine talking about life. That's why I love these men so much. They talk about real stuff. Sports is not their only issue, although it's still a big one. We drank merlot and took pictures of Ca and me in the middle of five cute guys. We were in heaven. I went to bed an hour ago but I couldn't fall asleep. Why did I plan a wedding? What . . . was I thinking? Did I think that I wanted all this attention?

I think not.

In my head I was reciting my wedding vows. When I wrote them weeks ago I thought they were brilliant, but tonight I think they suck. I had been asking Bill for the past two months to write his wedding vows. He told me today that he finally wrote his vows last night, while watching the Giants game! Did he at least write them during the commercials? That bothers me. But the thing that really bothers me is, his vows will probably be great.

Rick just came into the kitchen. He got stuck sleeping on the floor and he couldn't sleep either. I told him how afraid I was of tomorrow. He didn't know what to say so he shook his head in agreement and yawned. Men. I tucked him in my bed with Bill and I went to sleep with Ca in the other room. I finally fell asleep. My last thought was of Bill's face when he wakes up on his wedding day and finds Rick sleeping next to him.

Ha!

AUGUST 24

Well, we did it! We're officially married! It was quite a day, and one that got off to a rocky start. When the alarm went off at 6:00 A.M., of course Ca slept right through it. She's the only person I know that sets her snooze alarm, and *the real live time,* half an hour ahead, so she gets up on time. I pounced on her. She looked terrified, so then I got terrified. She's not supposed to *ever* look afraid! I went outside and paced around the garden in Grandpa's pajamas and found some inner calm that got me through the rest of the morning. Mr. Louie and Pucci arrived at 6:20 A.M. to pick up and organize the flowers. They have never been on time in all the years I've known them and today they were early. I was impressed and thankful. They were stressing out about not enough greenery at the altar and started digging all sorts of ivy and groundcover out near the redwood trees. It made me nervous, so I stayed out of it. Pucci looked like she was having a hard time, but every time she passed me she'd say, "Everything's going great! Just great. You relax." Then she'd go hyperventilate out in the backyard.

I finally let go. I let everyone else take charge and, while everyone else hustled and bustled around me, I sat there like a zombie, sipping coffee and deciding how much makeup to put on. I felt like an actress in a movie. Only I was ultra appreciative of everyone doing so much for me and I decided right then and there that I wouldn't put up with any more crying baby, millionaire, spoiled actors on my set.

So there!

The whole house was empty by 7:00 A.M. All the guys went out to Nicasio early to help place the flowers and help Dad, who had probably been there working since sunrise. An hour later, Pucci returned pretending everything was just fine, but then I heard her on the phone calling florists. I found out later that the wind was blowing over the sunflowers at the altar and she was trying to find something better to hold them up with. Ron called Ca a few minutes later to tell her that the goldfish were dying from the heat and they were having trouble getting them into the flower vases. He asked her: "Would it be better to forget the goldfish or would it be okay to have one or two dead goldfish blended into the floral arrangements?" I didn't want to hear any problems so I walked over to the drugstore and bought myself some Tums. I walked casually back home as if this were just another ordinary day in my life. I even pulled a few weeds and tossed a few snails as I came in the driveway, just to prove to myself that everything was perfectly normal. Ca was in the shower. I helped her get ready. Then I took a shower and she helped me get into the wedding-a-go-go outfit. She gave me a strapless bra and a thong to wear. (Yes, a thong. It drove me crazy all day long, and after the ceremony I went into the bathroom and ripped it right off.) Mindy arrived late, to put yet more makeup on me. She said I cursed her out for being late but I don't remember that. I had made a promise to myself that I wouldn't use the *F* word on my wedding day. I hope I didn't blow it so early. Then our best friend from childhood, Sue, came to drive us to the wedding and almost got us lost.

When we arrived in Nicasio all my fears went away. I was instantly surrounded by my girlfriends and felt safe. Then my mother came over looking beautiful, happy, and so proud. I walked indoors and immediately heard Sha, not in her indoor voice, bossing around the wedding party. She was lining them up for the procession and she showed no mercy! I still remember her yelling, "Move, go, yea you, *move* it." The only one to walk correctly stepping and stopping was our eight-year-old niece, Katie. Figures. My parents walked me down the aisle and I was beaming. Having my father on one side of me and my mother, leaning on me, on the other, was better than any dream I could've ever dreamed. We all held on so tightly to each other. I didn't want to ever let go.

The ceremony was long and it mixed a bunch of religions and world politics together. We stood under Grandpa Max's prayer shawl as the hoopa, surrounded by twenty-five gigantic sunflowers under the sweet California sky—Bill and me, two best friends for life. We had finally made it, made a commitment. Of course, the multi-cultural ceremony drove my mother crazy! I heard her off in the distance mumbling to herself, saying, "Oy. What is this? What is this mishmash? *Mashugene.* Oy!" Then, while Charlie was trying to light a candle in the wind, Ma said, "Annie stand up straight." My first thought was to turn around and glare, but then I heard my cousin Suzy, a true childhood comrade, laughing, and I started laughing too. At least she didn't say "Gigis out!" Ma was just being Ma, and if you look at it from a far off distance, like let's say, the moon . . . it *is* funny. Sort of.

We gave our personal vows and I told Bill that he was truly

the greatest gift of my life and that I would always cherish him. Of course, his vows were brilliant and he read them as if he were reciting Shakespeare.

At one point, when Charlie read the words of Gandhi "You must become the change that you are seeking," I looked over my shoulder to see my three sisters standing next to me with watery, smiling eyes where there used to be so much pain. For a moment I saw us all twenty-five years ago under Grandma's weeping willow tree. We were sweaty and glowing because Ga had just taught us how to do the twist. We were reading Archie comics, drinking colored syrup wax bottles from the corner dime store, and laughing because Sha had jinxed Ca. She had to shut up for a whole ten minutes!

Bill and I exchanged rings, stepped on the traditional glass together, hugged and kissed, and it was finally done. It's good there is someone taking pictures at your wedding, because it all goes by too fast and all the treasured moments blur together in your memory. I remember Mr. Louie threatening that we'd hear from his lawyer because his family wasn't on the A list. And I remember Jack and Dot huddled with a bunch of old high school friends, out near the horse stable. I passed by and it smelled like skunks. Jack was talking about a program he wants to start called "Seeds Across America." On one day of the year everyone all across America would go to a park and plant pot seeds.

Some things never change.

I remember Uncle Bob's speech. He introduced himself as the first person on earth to ever know me, since he delivered Ca and me to the world. He said some funny stuff. He had us all laughing. Then he went into his eighteen-minute recap of D day and the invasion at Normandy. We, who know him, just sat back and relaxed, knowing it would go on for a while. Newcomers stared in amazement and bewilderment!

My parents both made great speeches. Then Ga and a whole bunch of our friends got up and gave a piece of goodwill. Ron kind of floundered around up there; I'm still not sure what his point was.

Out on the dance floor, Bill was cutting the rug! I was dancing nearby when Dad came out on the floor with two big, brown bags filled with party goods. Let the festivities begin! He was handing out cowboy hats, party blowers, sunglasses, Hawaiian lei's, and plastic flowers to all of my friends. He looked just like Grandpa, when Grandpa would walk around at family holidays forcing chocolates into our pockets. It cracked me up. I went over to help him. He was right. Everyone loosened up and went wild.

After the wedding, we drove home in our flower-filled, lipstick, ribbon-and-balloon-covered Jeep. My sisters handed me a beautifully wrapped gift to open at the hotel for our wedding night. Why do I have the feeling it's the orange-striped sweater? I don't ever want to wash off the Just Married sign written in red lipstick on the rear window, because drivers were so nice to us today. All along the road people honked at us and waved. Why's everyone so nasty the rest of the time?

7 P.M.   It's sunset. The house is full of tipsy friends and relatives. On the radio, the Gospel station is blaring and the sisters are singing "This Little Light of Mine." I sneaked away behind the shed so that I could be alone and write down my thoughts. On the way, I passed my mother's peace rose and did a double take. It has a bud on it! No one will ever believe it. I started to write down how I was feeling. I don't want to forget how happy I am today, on my wedding day. I want proof that I once felt so loved and so elated.

I'd have to say that one of the most incredible moments of the day was when the band played Van Morrison's, "Have I Told You Lately That I Love You?" There they were, my parents, out on the dance floor, dancing together slowly. I watched them and all this forgiveness flushed through me. It hit me that they were just human and that they had tried as hard as they could. I think there's only so much you can blame your parents for, then you have to take responsibility for yourself and your own happiness. You finally wake up and realize that you do have a choice. If you face the past, you don't have to repeat it. You can dig yourself out of that cozy little rut you've dug yourself so comfortably into. You can either live your life angry and full of resentment or you can become the change you are seeking. Today my parents have grown up. I'm so proud of them! They may never know how much it meant to me to have them together, as friends, on my wedding day. I don't know what tomorrow will bring, but today, I know how lucky I am. Throughout the turbulent years of our childhood, there were so many glimpses of light and love that managed to shine through, and still do. This is what saved us. This is what heals us.